Chart
Sacred Geometry,
Sacred Space

Chartres

Sacred Geometry, Sacred Space

Gordon Strachan

with architectural drawings by
Oliver Perceval

Floris
Books

First published in 2003 by Floris Books

© 2003 Gordon Strachan
Fourth printing 2019

Gordon Strachan has asserted his right under the
Copyright, Designs and Patents Act 1988
to be identified as the Author of this Work

British Library CIP Data available
ISBN 978-086315-391-4
Printed in Great Britain by Bell & Bain Ltd

Contents

Acknowledgments 7

Introduction: The Sacred Site at Chartres 9

1. The Islamic Origin of the Pointed Arch 16

2. Sacred Geometry and Abbot Suger 35

3. St Bernard and the Early Gothic Plan 43

4. Of Cubes and Ka'aba 53

5. The Plan of Chartres 60

6. Dionysius the Areopagite and the Unknown God 74

7. St Denis, Chartres and the Darkness of God 88

Endnotes 103

Bibliography 107

Index 109

Photographic acknowledgments 111

Chronology

50	Dionysius the Areopagite (the first Dionysius) converted by St Paul in Athens. Tradition of Christian Platonism began.
90	Clement I, Bishop of Rome.
c.250	St Denis (the second Dionysius) Bishop of Paris, martyred.
c.335	Church of the Holy Sepulchre consecrated.
533	Pseudo-Dionysius (the third Dionysius), mystic theologian.
638	Muslims conquered Jerusalem.
692	Muslims completed the Dome of the Rock, Jerusalem.
715	Muslims completed El-Aksa Mosque, Jerusalem.
876	The Chemise of the Virgin. Important relic gifted to Chartres by Charles the Bald.
990	Fulbert at Chartres to 1028. The Cathedral School became famous throughout Europe.
1071	Seljuk Turks conquered Anatolia (Turkey) and threatened Constantinople.
1095	Council of Clermont: Pope Urban II preached the first Crusade in response to the Emperor of Constantinople's appeal for help against Seljuks.
1098	First Cistercian monastery at Cîteaux founded.
1099	Crusaders conquered Jerusalem.
1112	St Bernard (aged 22) joined the Cistercians.
1115	St Bernard appointed Abbot of Clairvaux.
1118	Knights Templars founded by Hugues de Payens as "The Order of the Poor Knights of Christ".
1122	Suger elected Abbot of St Denis, Paris.
1128	Council of Troyes: Templars officially recognized by Pope Honorius II.
1128–38	Geoffrey de Levès, Bishop of Chartres, accompanied St Bernard on journeys to Italy and Aquitain.
1130	Foundation of Sens Cathedral by Archbishop Henri de Sanglier (1122–42), friend of St Bernard.
1132	Abbot Suger began work on western façade at St Denis, Paris.
1134	Chartres: Fire; western towers rebuilding begun.
1140	Abbot Suger began rebuilding eastern apse at St Denis.
1144	Dedication of eastern apse in "The New Style" at St Denis.
1145	Chartres: Western (Royal) Portal begun.
1147	Second Crusade began.
1194	Chartres: Great fire; all destroyed except western towers and Portal; decision to rebuild in "The New Style".
1206	Chartres: South Porch installed.
1215	Chartres: High vaults erected.
1220–40	Chartres: Transcept rose-windows built.
1260	Chartres: Cathedral dedicated by King Louis IX.

Acknowledgments

I would like to thank Professor Keith Critchlow for first arousing my interest in Chartres cathedral and Professors Iain Boyd-White and Angus Macdonald for the opportunity to lecture on the early Gothic in the Department of Architecture at the University of Edinburgh.

Over recent years, I have been deeply indebted to many mature students who have attended my classes. They have shared my enthusiasm, lent me books, researched details and debated topics. Among these, I would particularly like to mention Sarah Frost, Pat Napier, Mary Catherine Burgess, Isabel Lennie, Andrew Gilmour and George Rankin.

Some years ago, I met with a group of friends to study the geometry of the Cathedral. It was led by the late Anne Macauley and Fred Robinson and included Maryel Gardyne, George Fraser, Alastair and Victoria Jack, Harry Bland and Jim Crockett. For the joy of our shared project and the task they left me to complete, I am very grateful.

There are others who have helped me to understand the meaning of sacred space; the late Robert Cowley and friends in the Research into Lost Knowledge Organisation (RILKO) in London, Jeanie Kar, Logan Lewis-Proudlock, Nick Bradford and students at the College of Psychic Studies (CPS) in London; Professors Jerome Murphy-O'Connor of the *École Biblique* and Doron Chen of the Hebrew University in Jerusalem; Professors Alastair Kee and Nicolas Wyatt in the Department of Religious Studies in Edinburgh University.

My thanks also go to all the staff in the Department of Architecture and the Centre for Continuing Education in Edinburgh University for their friendship and encouragement.

Above all I am grateful to Oliver Perceval who not only has been such a stimulating colleague, but has surveyed the key dimensions for geometrical analysis in plan and section by laser, and has then produced such excellent graphics and who has helped me to understand not only *how* Chartres Cathedral was built but also *why*.

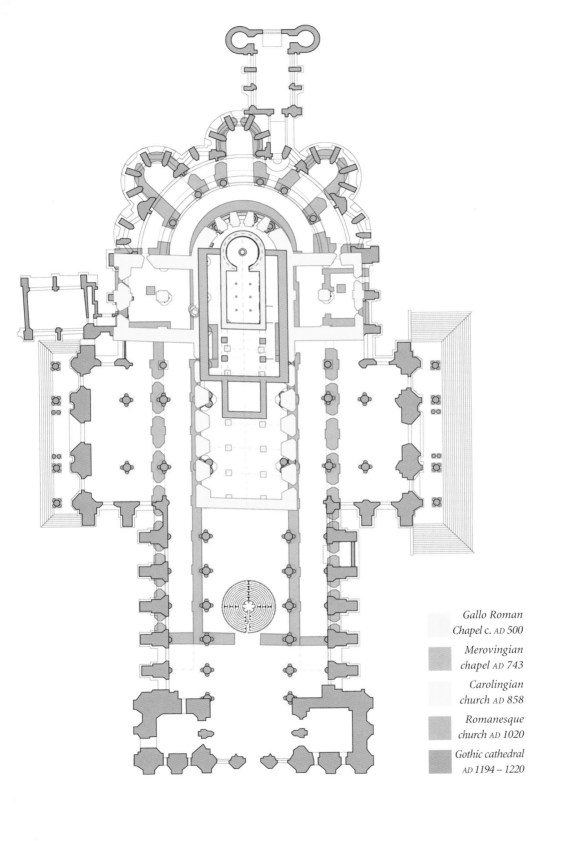

Gallo Roman
Chapel c. AD 500

Merovingian
chapel AD 743

Carolingian
church AD 858

Romanesque
church AD 1020

Gothic cathedral
AD 1194 – 1220

Introduction

THE SACRED SITE AT CHARTRES

There have been five known churches on the site of Chartres Cathedral, all of which have been destroyed by fire, except the last.[1] The Gothic masterpiece which we see today was built between 1194 and 1220 after a disastrous blaze which gutted almost the whole of the Romanesque church, excepting the two western towers erected earlier that century and also the Royal Portal, which had recently been built in the new Gothic style. This Romanesque church had been rebuilt in 1020, by Bishop Fulbert following an equally destructive conflagration. It was under Fulbert's brilliant leadership that the cathedral and its school became famous across Europe as a centre of learning, attracting such brilliant scholars as Thierry of Chartres, William of Conches and John of Salisbury.

The church before Fulbert's had been rebuilt by Bishop Gislebert in 858, after yet another catastrophe; this time a deliberate torching by Danish pirates. The church before Gislebert's was the original foundation which had also been the victim of arson in 743 at the hand of the Duke of Aquitaine. This, the earliest known church on the site, was built sometime between the fourth and sixth centuries and is known as the Gallo-Roman chapel. It is thought to have been modelled on the Church of the Holy Sepulchre which was built by the Emperor Constantine in the fourth century over the tomb where Jesus Christ was believed to have been buried and from which he rose from the dead — a church which featured most prominently at the time of the Crusades, as will be shown.

The ground plans of these five churches, based on archaeological research, fit inside each other like Russian dolls as shown opposite. Each of them rises like a phoenix from the ashes of its predecessor.[2] We may be thankful that, apart from a roof fire in 1836, there has been no serious threat to the present building for eight hundred years.

There is no hard evidence for any building on the site before

Since at least 100 BC the site at Chartres has been occupied and regarded as sacred. The diagram opposite shows the sequence of buildings that have inhabited the site from c. AD 500. These plans are largely drawn from archaeological surveys undertaken by Charles Stegeman in 1992.

the Gallo-Roman chapel but certain early literary sources have claimed that it was sacred to the Carnutes, a powerful Gaulish tribe, who had a Druid grotto dedicated to a pre-Christian virgin who they believed would conceive and bear a son. The similarity between this myth and the Christian story is held to account for the easy acceptance of the latter by the local pagan tribes. There was also a sacred well, the Well of the Strong Saints, which can still be seen in the crypt. It is near the statue and Gallery of Our Lady Under the Earth, whose veneration to this day, testifies to the general acceptance of this ancient link (see Chapter 1, illustrations on page 33f).[3]

There is also a legend that long before even the Druid grotto, there was a dolmen on the site dating back to megalithic times around 2000 BC.[4] No evidence whatsoever has been found for

The Carnutes Druid grotto.

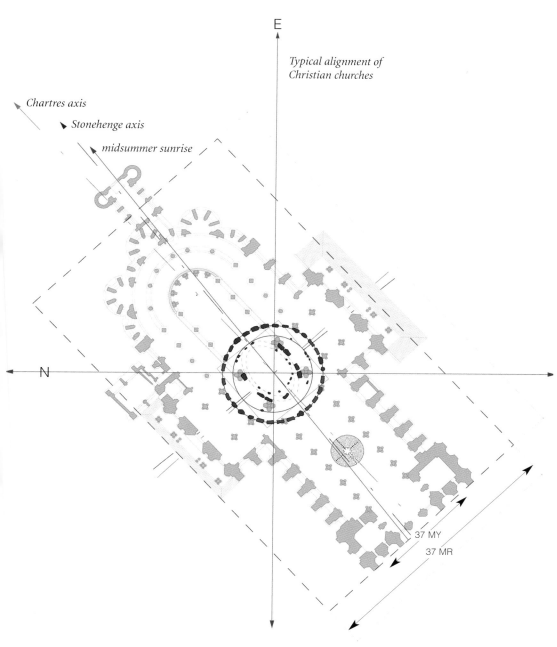

E

*Typical alignment of
Christian churches*

Chartres axis

Stonehenge axis

midsummer sunrise

N

37 MY

37 MR

*The orientation of the cathedral (47° E of N) in relation to Stonehenge (50.25°
E of N) and midsummer sunrise (51.58° E of N) is shown above. The outer
Sarsen ring of Stonehenge fits precisely within the outer pillars of the cathedral
crossing.
The cathedral is 37 Megalithic Rods (MR) wide and Stonehenge is 37 Megalithic
Yards (MY) wide (ratio of 2.5).*

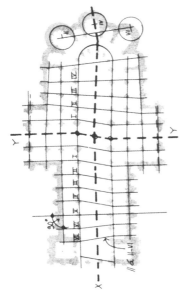

The two slightly different axes of the north and south spires which create a vibrato effect on the resonance of the Cathedral.

Pythagorean Comma at Stonehenge.

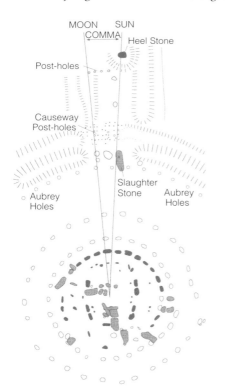

this, yet there are certain anomalies in the Gothic cathedral which are strangely reminiscent of megalithic monuments, particularly Stonehenge. First, its orientation is only fractionally different from Stonehenge, being close to midsummer sunrise[5] (page 11). This is radically different from the normal eastern orientation of churches and is probably unique in Christendom. Second, its north and south spires, so different in styles and heights, symbolize the sun and moon, as indicated by the solar and lunar symbols on their weather vanes. Their two complementary cycles are ingeniously built into the fabric of the design in the form of two slightly different axes, which run the length of the building, creating as it were, a *vibrato* effect on the resonance of the Cathedral. This is similar to the heelstone and causeway post holes at Stonehenge, which mark the difference between the longest day in the solar and lunar-metonic cycle. At Chartres this solar-lunar double axis causes a slight tilt over the length of the building, which can be easily observed when facing east from the west door.[6] It also accounts for the discrepancy between the South and the North Porches. In the South Porch, the outer columns lie a foot back from the top step of the platform, whereas in the North Porch they are flush with the second step down. Like the human face, the long and short axes of the building are both twisted to a slight but measurable extent which relates to the fraction known to the ancient and medieval world as the Pythagorean Comma.[7]

The third similarity between Chartres Cathedral and Stonehenge lies in the fact that, when they are measured in Megalithic units, they are found to be proportional to each other. This can be demonstrated by measuring them in Megalithic Yards (2.72 feet) and Megalithic Rods (6.8 feet) as proposed by Professor Alexander Thom. The mean diameter of the Sarsen circle is 37 Megalithic Yards,[8] while the full breadth of Chartres across the transepts is 2.5 times greater; namely 37 Megalithic Rods.[9] This is a very strange coincidence indeed, which together with the other similarities noted, while proving nothing, nevertheless raises very intriguing questions (see p.11).

However, fascinating though it would be to examine these anomalous coincidences more closely, it is not the purpose of this book to do so. These must be left to another occasion. It is

South Porch: column base is set over a foot behind the top step.

North Porch: column base is flush with the second riser down.

not possible to examine the entire complex history of the Chartres site in one small volume! It is the intention of *this* book to concentrate only on the final, finished masterpiece, which we see today and to answer the specific question: why did the builders of Gothic Chartres bother to expend such a huge amount of energy and skill not just on rebuilding but on changing it from the Romanesque to the Gothic style? Was it in response to changing fashion? Was it a result of competition with other cities? Was it an expression of the new urban independence from feudalism and the affluence it brought? Was it the need for a larger sanctuary to cope with the new epoch of spiritual zeal?

Given that the answer was probably a combination of each of these, the question still remains, where did the Gothic style itself come from, and why was it so important? Did it emerge from the Romanesque world through the trial and error of inspired Norman and Burgundian masons? Was it the result of indigenous genius or did it come from somewhere else? Was it imported and, if so, from where?

I believe that it came, to a large extent, from outside Europe and that it was the product of a unique blending of indigenous building skills with the architectural genius of Islam. I also believe that this can be demonstrated by tracing the origin of the Gothic, or *pointed*, arch back to the traditional Islamic architecture of the Middle East, as it was discovered by French Crusaders in the late eleventh and early twelfth centuries.

Although it was not my intention that this book should have a wider, topical relevance, my years of research have coincided strangely with those in which Islam has become increasingly viewed as a common enemy of the West. I cannot help noticing that this is strikingly similar to the political situation in Europe in the late eleventh century, which led to the First Crusade, and that this is the exact historical location of the story I am about to tell!

I believe that the current demonizing of Islam is largely propaganda promoted for political purposes. Perhaps if we were not so ignorant of Islam — its history, faith and culture — we would see how much we are being manipulated. For there is another side to Islam, a side which is tolerant, inclusive, cultured and spiritual. It is this side which some of the Crusaders discovered after they conquered Jerusalem in 1099, to the immense benefit of the West. It is this side which we need to rediscover for ourselves today in order that we do not fall victim to collective western prejudice, and so that our supposed common enemy might become our common friend. If this book can help in this process then it will have achieved something of more importance than its original intention.

Chapter 1

THE ISLAMIC ORIGIN
OF THE POINTED ARCH

The pointed arch is the most distinctive feature of the Gothic style, marking it out from all earlier styles in western architecture, including the Romanesque which immediately preceded it. Before the rise of the Gothic in the twelfth century, almost all arches were round, and had been since Roman times. Flying buttresses, pinnacles, stained glass and rose windows are also distinctive Gothic innovations, but the pointed arches and interior cross-ribbed vaults remain the most obvious and important characteristics of the Gothic style.

Despite the general acceptance that this is so, it is surprising that there is no consensus as to where the pointed arch came from. In fact, for a long time, there has been a lively debate among scholars as to its origin. Some have said that it evolved gradually out of the Romanesque, by a process of trial and error, as master masons sought to improve their technical skills.[1] Others have maintained that it came from outside northern Europe, from Islamic influences in Spain, Sicily and the Middle East.[2]

I believe that it did indeed come from Islamic sources and I do so for two reasons: first, because the particular *types* of pointed arch used in early Gothic are the same as those which had already been used in Islamic architecture for a long time; and second, because it is doubtful whether there was sufficient knowledge of geometry within Europe in the early twelfth century to cope with the more complex geometrical calculations, which pointed arches and cross-ribbed vaulting demanded.

Correspondence between notable scholars in the eleventh century has shown that they didn't know how to solve very simple geometrical problems, whereas by the thirteenth century their successors did, which is obvious in the early thirteenth-century sketchbook of the master mason, Villard de Honnecourt. This advance in learning could only have come from Islam during the twelfth century following cultural contact in Spain at inter-faith centres such as Toledo and Cordova, and from the Crusades which started with the conquest of Jerusalem in 1099.[3] Today it is difficult for us in the West to realize that in those times, Islam had achieved a far higher level of civilization than north-western Europe, in almost every field of the arts and sciences. However, the historical evidence clearly indicates that it was only through contact with Islam that the full works of Plato, Aristotle and Euclid, which had been largely lost in the West, were rediscovered. It was only after these, and other, classical works had been fully translated from Arabic into Latin, and added to the curriculum in the schools of Paris, Laon, Chartres and the other centres of learning, that a renaissance of culture was triggered off in northern France. The rise of Gothic architecture was the most spectacular result of this.[4]

This is the only obvious explanation for the pervasive and proficient use of geometry throughout Villard de Honnecourt's sketchbook. It is also the reason why one of his compass drawings gives us a vital clue as to the origin of the pointed arch. Drawing 57 (below) in Honnecourt's book demonstrates: "How to make three kinds of arches with a single opening of the compass." This drawing is extremely revealing because, as can be seen in the illustration, two of these arches are pointed. The one drawn above the line has a span divided into three and the one below the line into two.

Villard de Honnecourt's compass drawing of pointed arches.

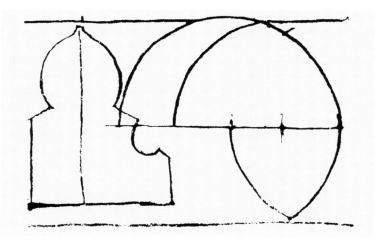

Villard de Honnecourt does not say where these simple but very "Gothic" arches came from, but there is reason to believe that the arch, whose span is divided into three, came from mosques in western Syria, in what is now eastern Turkey. The evidence for this comes from the work of Professor K.A.C. Creswell, the great architectural historian of the Middle East. He noticed that the arches in early Muslim architecture were not as pointed as they became in later centuries. He observed that from the sixth to eighth centuries, the gap between the two centres from which the arches were drawn was no more than one-tenth of the full width or span of the arches, but during the ninth and tenth centuries, it had moved through one-seventh to one-fifth and even occasionally to one-third, as the illustration shows.[6]

The right-hand "one-third" arch is exactly the same as Villard de Honnecourt's, thus demonstrating its Islamic derivation.

This being so, two questions arise. First, where were these Islamic arches originally seen and, second, who brought back to western Europe the knowledge of how to build them?

The most persuasive answer to the first of these questions comes from the medieval architectural historian, John Harvey, who maintains that they were seen by the First Crusaders as they marched through western Syria in 1097, on their way to the Holy Land. It was there that they met and fought the Seljuk Turks. The Seljuks had recently conquered the whole area and were advancing on Constantinople, the capital of eastern Christendom. The First Crusade was launched in 1096 for the express purpose of stopping this happening and re-opening the pilgrim routes to Palestine, which the Seljuks had closed. As the Seljuks advanced west they built magnificent new mosques at

Early Islamic arches as analysed by Prof. K.A.C. Creswell.

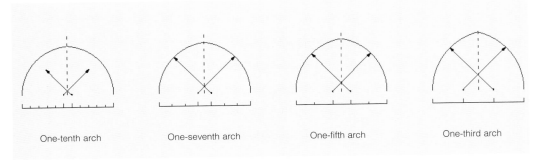

| One-tenth arch | One-seventh arch | One-fifth arch | One-third arch |

CHARTRES: SACRED GEOMETRY, SACRED SPACE

Diyarkbakir, Gazientep, Siirt and Bitlis, where the Crusaders would have seen good examples of various types of pointed arch.[7]

The answer to the second question — who brought back the knowledge to build them? — is more complex and, I believe, happened in two phases. First, it started with victorious Crusaders bringing captured masons home with them. One such was Lalys, whom Richard de Granville brought back to build Neath Abbey in Glamorganshire, and who later became architect to Henry I, the Norman king of England.[8] Similarly the dating of early examples of cross-ribbed vaulting at Durham Cathedral coincides with the return of the Prince-Bishop of Durham, William of St Calais, in the mid 1190s. His successful campaign against the Muslims in Sicily resulted in him bringing back captured Islamic masons.[9]

The second phase began when Muslim expertise had been mastered sufficiently by local European masons, so that no more dependence on captured craftsmen was necessary. It is difficult to say when this took place precisely, but it was

probably a gradual process. However, there does appear to have been a particular moment when indigenous craftsmen were considered to be fully equipped and self-sufficient in their Islamic expertise, and when the pointed arch and the cross-ribbed vault could be launched officially as the *Gothic* or, as it was simply called at the time "the New Style."[10] This was in 1144 when Abbot Suger of the Abbey of St Denis, just outside Paris, dedicated the newly-completed Eastern Apse of his church. He had had it rebuilt in the Islamic style, with slender columns and walls capped with pointed arches which were all "one-fifth" arches as in Professor Creswell's illustration. Abbot Suger was the leading figure in Church and state in France at the time and so had the authority to call all the nobles and bishops to the official ceremony of dedication in the name of the King, in support of the Capetian dynasty. Amongst those present was Bernard, Abbot of Clairvaux. Suger and St Bernard knew each other well and the latter's presence was an endorsement of his achievement.[11] The result was that the New Style began to spread rapidly round France as if by royal, as well as ecclesiastical, decree. One of the first to respond to this call was the Bishop of Chartres, Geoffrey de Levès, who had been at the dedication of St Denis and who, in 1145, began rebuilding a new Western Portal in the New Style.

CHARTRES: SACRED GEOMETRY, SACRED SPACE

It had three large doors, each surmounted by an Islamic one-fifth arch.

How had this come about? How had the architectural style of the conquered Islamic "infidels" in the space of forty-four years, become endorsed by the French aristocracy and ecclesiastical hierarchy and proclaimed officially as the style of the new Christian cultural renaissance and spiritual revival? In order to answer this, we must go back to the conquest of Jerusalem by the First Crusaders in 1099 and outline the change of outlook which, I believe, took place in the minds and hearts of some of them as they became the resident garrison in the Holy City.

The Sufis and the Templars

As already mentioned, the objectives of the First Crusade were to protect Constantinople from the advancing Seljuk Turks and to re-open the pilgrim routes to Christian sacred sites, of which the Church of the Holy Sepulchre was considered to be the most sacred. This was the Church originally built in 335 by the Emperor Constantine over the site of the tomb in which Christ had been buried, and from which he had risen from the dead. It had also been extended to house the presumed site of the Rock of Calvary on which he had been crucified by the Romans. The liberation of this particular church from Muslim

Chartres: the Western Portal showing "one fifth" Islamic arches of the "New Style."

The Dome of the Rock.

captivity was the ultimate military goal and spiritual aspiration of the Crusaders.

The shock of being so quickly successful in achieving all this left something of a vacuum in the consciousness of these militant Christians, most of whom returned home. As the three hundred who stayed turned themselves into an army of occupation, they had time to get to know their conquered enemy. As today, the old city of Jerusalem was not large, so they lived at close quarters with those Jews and Muslims whom they had not slaughtered on arrival. Indeed they must have got to know the political and religious leaders of the Jewish and Muslim communities in order to maintain effective law and order. In doing so they would have come across the Sufis — the esoteric, mystical Muslim movement — who are known to have been in Jerusalem and were enjoying something of a revival throughout Islam at that time.[12] They would have heard about the recent sojourn of the most famous Sufi teacher of the day, al-Ghazali, who had come to the Sufi school after resigning his professorship in Islamic law in Baghdad, in order to experience God rather than just *know about* him.[13]

CHARTRES: SACRED GEOMETRY, SACRED SPACE

The occupiers would have been shown round the Haram el Sharif, the Temple Mount, and discovered that it was the third most sacred site in Islam after Mecca and Medina. They must have marvelled at the architectural brilliance of the Dome of the Rock, built after the Muslims first conquered Christian Jerusalem between 688 and 692, and obviously so much more beautiful than their own Church of the Holy Sepulchre. They learned that the protruding rock, around and over which it was built, was sacred to the Muslims because they believed that it was from there that Muhammad had made his famous night journey, or *mystical ascent*, to heaven, and that the Aksa Mosque, the other building on the Temple Mount, was so called because its name indicated that this was as far as Muhammad had travelled from his headquarters at Mecca.

The Christians would have been impressed by the exotic pointed arches especially those in the Aksa Mosque, which in Arabic were called *mukhammas* arches, meaning "divided into five," because they were constructed by dividing the span of the arch into five and then drawing the arcs from points 2 and 3, as in Professor Creswell's illustration (page 24).

The Church of the Holy Sepulchre.

El Aksa Mosque.

The invaders no doubt visited the workshops, which taught craftsmen how to build these arches and mosques whose proportions enhanced their beauty and sanctity, and created an atmosphere conducive to prayer and meditation. They would have been told that, according to Islamic principles of sacred architecture, the round Roman and Romanesque arch was considered to be un-spiritual, leading from earth to earth whereas the pointed arch was considered to be spiritual because it led upwards from both sides, from earth to air and beyond to heaven; that the arch itself, because it echoed the shape of the subtle body of the worshipper, was therefore believed to help adjust the balance of the aura.

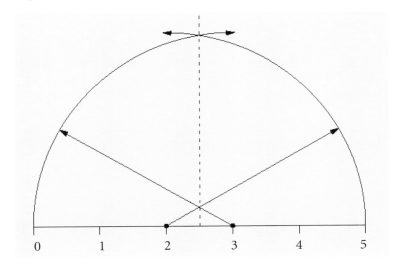

A "one-fifth"
mukhammas *arch.*

CHARTRES: SACRED GEOMETRY, SACRED SPACE

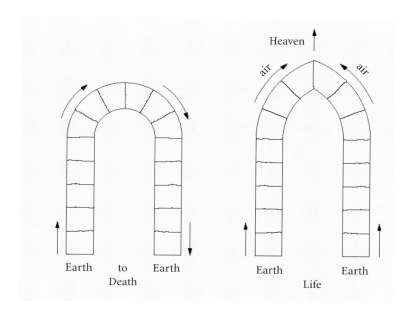

Heaven

air — air

Earth to Earth   Earth   Earth
Death
Life

They discovered fairly soon that the Sufis not only honoured the person of Jesus as one of the seven sages of Islam, like all good Muslims, but that they were also committed to an inter-faith pluralism, which believed that every religion contained some important aspects of the one universal truth. Thus, among the erstwhile conquering warriors, those who were devout Christians would have been amazed to meet tolerant, friendly Sufis who, though Muslims, appeared to be as much at home with the Jewish and Christian scriptures as with their own. I believe that their unprecedented exposure to this toler-ant, Sufi pluralism, worked a profound change on the minds and hearts of a number of sensitive, spiritual Crusaders, and that they became converted to the inclusive mystical path which the Sufis represented. I believe they made a conscious decision to learn from these wise and enlightened Muslim teachers.

This is the only way in which I can account for the relative secrecy surrounding the rise of the Templars and the major role they must have played in the transmission of Muslim architec-tural expertise from the Middle East to northern France, which eventually made the skills of captured Islamic craftsmen redundant and opened the way for the rise of the Gothic on an international scale.

In Jeruralem in 1118 the Templars were founded by Hugues

The pointed arch was felt by Muslims to be more uplifting than the rounded arch.

de Payens as "The Order of the Poor Knights of Christ," and were confirmed as an order of warrior monks by Pope Honorius II, at the Council of Troyes in 1128. After this their official title became the Order of Poor Knights of Christ and the Temple of Solomon. They had evolved out of many unofficial meetings over many years between certain high ranking Crusaders and high ranking aristocrats and churchmen in northern France. This had begun in 1104 when Hugues, Count of Champagne, was told by a returning Crusader about the impact the Sufis were having on some of the resident garrison in Jerusalem. The subsequent to-ing and fro-ing of Count Hugues and other notable knights led to a growing realization that some organization should be set up at the highest level, to channel the Sufi wisdom back to France.[14]

The official purpose of the first Templars — and there were only nine of them — was to keep the roads in the Holy Land free for pilgrims. They were all high-born, educated, intelligent and spiritual men with wide European connections. Their leader, or Grand Master, was Hugues de Payens who held land north-west of Troyes. His second in command was Godefroy de Saint-Omer, a Fleming. Another was André de Montbard, uncle to St Bernard, the Abbot of Clairvaux and leader of the Cistercian monastic order. Payen de Montdidier, Archambaud de Saint-Aignan, André de Gundomare, Roral, Godefroy and Geoffroy Bisol were the others. Although they were called "poor knights" they were all far from poor, yet it is probable that they did attempt to keep their monastic vow of poverty as well as those of celibacy and obedience, which St Bernard had drawn up for them in 1129.

The most important clue that the Templars' mission was not only to guard the pilgrim routes but also to learn from the Sufis, lies in the symbolism of the number nine. When the Order was founded in 1118, there were only nine knights, which is strange because it is obvious that nine were far too few to be effective as protectors of pilgrims. Even more odd is the fact that no more knights were added for a further nine years. Because of this, some authors have proposed that their real job was to dig under the Temple Mount for ancient documents, which would reveal some shocking, suppressed truth about Jesus, or would lead to the discovery of some priceless relic such as the Ark of the Covenant.

I confess that I have serious reservations about such theories because, quite apart from flimsy evidence, they assume that the Templars were not devout Christians under monastic discipline, who, however misguided we may consider them to have been, were, at least, genuinely concerned about spiritual as well as military matters.[15] Consequently, what is overlooked, is the fact that they were already undergoing a profoundly spiritual and personal experience, as distinct from a political or heretical one. This derived from their encounters with the Sufis and other Islamic scholars whose knowledge included the higher spiritual dimension of *gnosis.*

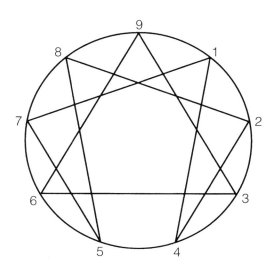

The Enneagram symbolizing aspects of nine character types in Sufi teaching.

Yet this is, I believe, what is implied if the symbolism of the number nine is taken seriously. For nine is the number of that aspect of Sufi teaching known as the *Enneagram,* which is a tool for a system of psycho-spiritual development based on nine character types. Its importance and effectiveness can be gauged by the fact that it is still in widespread use today in Christian circles concerned with psychological and spiritual growth. The number nine was also extremely important in the "Nine Degrees of Wisdom" of the esoteric Shiite Ismailis who were very strong in Persia and Syria at that time and who the Crusaders encountered in the 1130s when they were given their first important frontier march in the Amanus Mountains, north of Antioch.[16]

The number nine was equally important in the twelfth century to Christians because it was the number of celestial hierarchies in the mystical theology of Dionysius the Areopagite who, since his writings had been translated from Greek into Latin in the ninth century, had been known in western Christendom by those who wanted to follow a more mystical path of spiritual development. Its importance at St Denis and Chartres is explained in Chapters 6 and 7. Nine had also been most significant in western education since the tenth century because it was the number of Aristotle's *Categories.* These categories, which were thought to encompass all the ways in which objects could be analysed were: quantity, quality, relation, position, place, time, state, action and affection.[17]

So the fact that there were only nine Templars for the first nine years, can best be understood as a code, not for digging up heretical documents, or ancient relics, but for learning from Islamic higher education what the two outwardly warring faiths had inwardly in common; for discovering and sharing this common, spiritual heritage; for growing in knowledge and experience of spiritual things; and for gaining an understanding of, and expertise in, craftsmanship. The really shocking revelation with which they had to come to terms, was the trauma of meeting men who made them feel culturally inferior, intellectually unlearned and spiritually shallow. This was a far more profoundly disturbing experience than the discovery of any heretical document, for this was life-changing at the core of their being. They might continue to win more battles with the sword but they could hardly begin to compete with the conquered enemy in matters of culture, education and the spiritual life.

I am aware that my theory has probably condemned me to the company of fantasists and charlatans in the eyes of some academic historians of the Templars and the Crusades. However, their meticulous scholarship is directed almost entirely towards the details of military, political and ecclesiastical history, and says very little about cultural exchange.[18] My theory concerns the probable Islamic origins of Gothic architecture and is not without its exponents among reputable architectural historians.

While the rest of the Crusaders continued to engage with the military might of Islam, the first Templars acknowledged that they had found the source of much of the learning which had long been taught in the Cathedral schools back home, such as at Laon, Paris and especially Chartres.[19] They were excited, not so much by the realization that they had much in common such as the legacy of Pythagoras, Plato, Aristotle, Euclid and Ptolemy, but by the fact that Sufi and Islamic scholars had taken their studies to a more advanced level.[20] Also, owing to the Islamic practice of *akbar jahd*, the greatest effort, scholars were prepared to share this knowledge. As a result of this openness, the first Templars learnt about Islam's more advanced, spiritually-integrated form of architecture. However, they were then faced with a profound dilemma. On the one hand, they were being transformed by what they were learning in the relatively peaceful period up to 1144 but on the other hand, after the fall

El Aksa Mosque: The three central bays which were actually built by the Templars, or at least under their supervision, in the early twelfth century.

Chartres Cathedral: West Portal, begun 1145 using "one fifth" arches, the same as those identified at El Aksa Mosque above.

of Edessa, they were plunged once again into war with the Muslims.[21]

How was this problem to be overcome? By reinforcing the Templars' role as an elite order of warrior monks whose military mission was to defend the Holy places but whose spiritual secret mission was to learn all they could at this higher level and to transmit it back to France; though only to an educated aristocratic and ecclesiastical few, not to the many, lest their secret might be discovered.[22] Although this learning was thus transmitted to the few, it cannot be considered to have been heresy, nor was it even esoteric or occult in the strict sense. For to carry education in the liberal arts and sciences from primary to secondary and then tertiary level, only appears to be esoteric or occult to the uneducated and ignorant. Likewise to move from a theology based on doctrine to one based more on mystical experience, is not heretical, just a change of emphasis, which many considered to be long overdue.

There can be little doubt that such a change took place. Its expression can be traced through the spectacular rise of the cult of St Denis, and the understanding of the mystical theology of Dionysius the Areopagite, as will be outlined later. That the Templars graduated from their studies in the sacred architecture of Islam with flying colours can also be seen in the three central arches of the porch of the Aksa Mosque on the Temple Mount.

Architectural analysis of the three central bays of el Aksa has revealed that they were actually built by the Templars or at least under their supervision during the time when they made it their headquarters.[23] They were built according to the principles of Islamic sacred architecture and were regarded as having been accurately constructed, which is confirmed by the decision of Saladin, the general of the Muslim army who, when he reconquered Jerusalem in 1187, pulled down all Crusader buildings in the vicinity, but not these three bays. He left them standing, as they still stand today, flanked by two more bays on either side, which were added later under the Mameluke dynasty[24] (page 29 top).

By 1187, however, the earlier successes of the Crusaders had changed to a series of crushing defeats as Saladin's brilliant generalship re-asserted Islamic authority throughout the land. But in the meantime, the Templars' secret mission had been

The Templar cross as the halo of Christ on the West Portal of Chartres cathedral (see also photo page 71).

successful back in France. By the 1130s much of the higher knowledge and deeper spirituality had been transmitted to leaders of Church and state. Teams of masons were rapidly becoming proficient in constructing pointed arches and cross-ribbed vaults. Around 1130, St Bernard persuaded the Archbishop of Sens to rebuild his cathedral according to an integrated plan and elevation based on what was becoming known as "the New Style" (see Chapter 3).[25] In 1140, Abbot Suger of St Denis decided to rebuild his Eastern Apse and choir in the new Islamic style, which was finished and dedicated in 1144 when the New Style was officially inaugurated. At the official inauguration many of the great and the good were inspired to espouse the new movement. Among these was the Bishop of Chartres, Geoffrey de Levès, who as stated began to build his famous Western Portal in 1145. In this Portal he designed three pointed arches, all one-fifth *mukhammas* arches, exactly the same as those in the porch of el Aksa (page 29). A comparison of the two buildings makes this obvious but most scholars have either missed or denied it.[26] Yet, as mentioned, architectural archaeology has confirmed the Templar origin of the Aksa porch and a knowledge of symbolism confirms the Templar influence at Chartres. For on the nimbus or halo round the huge sculpture of Christ in the central tympanum of the central arch, is the outline of a cross. There are many different types of cross in Christian iconography, each of which carries its own symbolic meaning and there is no mistaking the unique curving arms of this one, for these are unmistakably the curved arms of the Templar Cross — *la croix pattée* — which declares to all who know the symbolism, that the Templars were resoundingly successful in the accomplishment of their secret mission.[27]

Some years later, in the early thirteenth century, when the new cathedral was built out of the ashes of the fire of 1194, similar porches were constructed on the newly-added North and South Transepts. Each had three doors surmounted by three one-fifth Islamic *mukhammas* arches, together making nine doors with nine arches in all. Thus was further emphasized the spiritual heritage which linked the Sufis, the Templars and the mystical theology of Dionysius the Areopagite.

In addition, it must be noted that nine is also the number of the Triple Goddess of the ancient indigenous religion of the Celtic North and that the earliest legend from the time of the Carnutes at Chartres, as noted, speaks of a Druid grotto and a well sacred to a pre-Christian Celtic virgin who would conceive and bear a son. This virgin was later called Our Lady

The Southern Tympanum of the Western Portal. This sculpture is understood to be of Mary as Sedes Sapientiae, *the Seat or Source of Wisdom and of Jesus as the* Logos, *the incarnate Word. Round them are sculptured figures representing the Seven Liberal Arts with their muses.*

CHARTRES: SACRED GEOMETRY, SACRED SPACE

Under the Earth; the gallery, the chapel in the crypt, and the nearby well are dedicated to her to this day.[28] It is also said that although the present wooden sculpture of her there is a replica of one lost in the sixteenth century, the original was the prototype for the twelfth century mason who sculpted the massive Virgin and Child on the Southern Tympanum of the new Western Portal. This sculpture is understood to be of Mary as *Sedes Sapientiae*, the Seat or Source of Wisdom and of Jesus as the Logos, the incarnate Word. Round them are sculptured figures representing the Seven Liberal Arts with their muses.

It is easy to see how readily the Sufi, Templar and Dionysian wisdom could be embraced by the cult of Our Lady Under the Earth, who re-emerged in the twelfth century as the Black Virgin, with strong Druidic and Celtic connections.[29] It is also easy to see how readily all these could be embraced by, and enfolded within, a pluralist interpretation of and deeper devotion to the already popular cult of the Blessed Virgin Mary, to whom the cathedral is officially dedicated. For the cult of the Blessed Virgin had always been strong at Chartres.

Left:
The Druidic Well of the Strong, still venerated in the crypt of the cathedral.

Right:
The wooden sculpture of Our Lady Under the Earth in the crypt chapel.

Her *chemise*, said to have been worn at the birth of Jesus, had been the cathedral's most treasured relic since 876, and made the place famous as a pilgrim centre. When it was miraculously preserved from the fire of 1194 it proved its potency once again by becoming the agent of a new enthusiasm to rebuild. The cathedral we see today could in a sense, be said to be not only built in her honour, but also by her inspiration. It was she, together with the Triple Goddess, who united Muslim, Christian and Celtic wisdom into a joint, creative "greatest effort," which still stands as an inspiration to people of many faiths in our modern pluralist world.

Chapter 2

SACRED GEOMETRY
AND ABBOT SUGER

For some years the subject of Sacred Geometry has been enjoying a revival, particularly in Britain since being embraced by H.R.H. Prince Charles and his School of Architecture. A certain mystique surrounds it and yet it can be defined quite simply as the geometry of Euclid, used for symbolic purposes, in the service of traditional and sacred architecture.

It is appropriate that it should become fashionable in our postmodern world, for its pedigree goes back a long way, to the pyramids of Egypt, the ziggurats of Mesopotamia, Hindu temples and Islamic mosques. In the Judaic tradition it began as early as the time of Moses, when he was told to make a holy tent, or tabernacle, according to the measurements which he had been shown by God on Mount Sinai, and to the measurements of the Temple of Solomon, whose proportions were given by Yahweh to King David.

In the early centuries of Christianity, this tradition from Moses and Solomon was grafted onto the Greek philosophy of numbers and geometric proportions, as propounded by the great Greek philosophers, Pythagoras and Plato. Hebrew and Greek cultures thus combined to create what is known as Christian Platonism.

There were four subjects, all connected to numbers, which formed an important part of this new synthesis: arithmetic which was pure number; music, or harmonics, which was number in time; geometry which was number in space; and astronomy-astrology which was number in space-time. Together these were known as the *Quadrivium*. Although Greek in origin they were absorbed into the educational system of the Christian monasteries and Cathedral schools, and were taught as four of the Seven Liberal Arts throughout the Middle Ages, as mentioned in the previous chapter.[1]

However, despite this great heritage of Christian Platonism, which played such a crucial role in the rise of the Gothic style, since the nineteenth century there has been considerable resistance to the idea that geometrical symbolism played any significant part in the calculations of medieval masons. John Ruskin has much to answer for in this connection because, despite his passion for the Gothic, he taught that the rich variety of proportions, which he had observed, were not the result of any *system* of proportions but of exactly the opposite — of a "fixed scorn" and "contempt" for any accuracy in measurement. He insisted that the master masons built "altogether from feeling."[2]

This paradoxical position greatly appealed to William Morris. So much so that it became something of a dogma in the Arts and Crafts Movement, epitomizing the rugged, creative, individual spirit of the true craftsman. Echoes of this can still be found. For instance, in *A Guide to Architectural Styles* Herbert Pothorn claims that "Gothic builders took little account of exact dimensions" but "they did have an instinct for proportions of dimensions."[3]

For "instinct" read "feeling" and it echoes Ruskin exactly. Likewise in a Pitkin Guide, *Cathedral Architecture*, Martin Briggs goes even further when he contends that: "The idea that a church was and is planned intentionally in the shape of a cross to remind us of Christ's crucifixion, is now generally rejected by some learned scholars." He adds: "The old idea that the tall spire was a finger pointing to heaven is now discounted."[4]

I can only comment that if such an opinion had been expressed during the building of Chartres, it would probably have ended with a nasty accident from the highest scaffolding!

It would be quite wrong, however, to paint a completely negative picture, for there have been a number of valiant attempts to explain the Gothic in terms of geometrical analyses. In the nineteenth century there were such men as Billings, Cockerell, Penrose, Papworth and, most notably, Viollet-le-Duc, who clearly criticized Ruskin. Viollet-le-Duc said: "it would be self-deception to imagine that proportions in architecture are governed by instinct. There are absolute rules and geometrical principles."[5]

Nevertheless, none of these met with widespread acceptance and in 1904 William Lethaby, himself an authority on the subject,[6] expressed a general mood of weariness when he confessed: "It is vain to look, as many have done, for any general doctrines of proportion."[7] B.G. Morgan, in *Canonic Design*, comes to the same opinion with regard to similar twentieth-century efforts made by such leading architectural historians as Moessel, Ghyka, Jouven, Levy, Lesser and Funk-Hellet, saying that, stimulating though they are, they "leave us still without an authoritative theory."[8]

Morgan's concluding summary is worth careful consideration because, although written in 1961, before the current revival of interest in Sacred Geometry began, he still speaks for the most widely-held opinion among scholars today. He says that although masonry work demanded geometrical knowledge, the master masons of the Gothic period were not much interested in anything beyond the practical problems of their trade:

> This is not to imply that the geometrical procedures adopted by the master-masons were quite devoid of symbolical or metaphysical overtones, but rather to suggest that such procedures were *essentially* generated by the need to solve practical problems of building, and any metaphysical connotations associated with them were acquired adventitiously in the course of time and were superfluous to their basic nature and purpose. Consequently, to attempt to deduce the nature of medieval design practices from a consideration of symbolic accretions is to deal with the shadow and not with the substance.[9]

Morgan is entitled to his opinion but, like other critics of symbolic geometry, he does not seem to have heard of Plato or of the Platonism which permeated the minds of the Gothic founders. Had he done so, he would have known that his argument is back to front and upside down; particularly in his use of the words *essentially, substance* and *real*. For instance, when he claims that "to attempt to deduce the nature of medieval design practices from a consideration of their symbolic accretions is to deal with the shadow and not the substance," he would have been howled down by Abbot Suger, St Bernard and

Another aspect of nineness?

the master masons of the New Style. For them, as for Plato, it was not the symbolic or metaphysical that was the shadow, nor was it the practical considerations of the masons which were the substance. Following Plato, it was the metaphysical which was the real, and it was the material world which was the shadow. This is obvious from the writings of Suger and can be summed up in the famous credo of his symbolic aesthetics which was so wonderfully exemplified in his New Style at St Denis:

> Thus when — out of my delight in the beauty of the house of God — the loveliness of the many-coloured gems has called me away from the external cares, and worthy meditation has induced me to reflect, trans- ferring that which is material to that which is immaterial, on the diversity of the sacred virtues: then it seems to me that I see myself dwelling, as it were, in some strange region of the universe which neither exists entirely in the slime of the earth nor entirely in the purity of heaven; and that, by the grace of God, I can be transported from this inferior to that higher world in an anagogical manner.[10]

By "anagogical manner" Suger meant that when we are in reflective meditation, the beauty of the material objects, which we see in the church, leads us on to see *through* them and to perceive their spiritual counterparts in the unseen, immaterial world. In this progression, earthly objects are transformed. They are still there and it is important that they are, but by means of this anagogical process, we are led to see them in what we might call their *archetypal* form. We are transported to an intermediate place where our consciousness is neither com- pletely material nor completely spiritual, but is both at the same time.

This is the language of Christian Platonism in which mate- rial objects are symbolic of their spiritual archetypes. It is also the language of mysticism because Suger is ultimately speak- ing about an experience of the divine within the material, of the symbols partaking of that which they symbolize. He is talking about what today we might call "an altered state of con- sciousness."

It seems to be implied in one of his own poems — which he

had inscribed on the doors of his new West Porch — that he intended us to have something like a mystical experience in his new church. In the poem he encourages us to admire the wonderful craftsmanship and let it brighten our minds to help us travel on to see Christ as the True Door. Thus "The dull mind rises to truth through that which is material." The words "travel" and "rises" imply a journey, a process, a transformation:

> Whoever thou art, if thou seekest to extol the glory of these doors,
> Marvel not at the gold and the expense, but at the craftsmanship of the work.
> Bright is the noble work; but, being nobly bright, the work
> Should brighten the minds, so that they may travel through the true lights
> To the True Light where Christ is the true door,
> In what manner it be inherent in this world the golden door defines:
> The dull mind rises to truth through that which is material
> And, seeing this light, is resurrected from its former submersion.[11]

It would appear that Suger's intention is made abundantly clear in his poem. If we take him at his word, then the purpose of his rebuilding and the New Style was to help brighten the minds of whoever entered, so that "they might travel through the true lights to the True Light where Christ is the true door." He does not say that the New Style should be admired for its own sake, or that it has — as the austere St Bernard feared — been lavishly embellished with silver, gold and precious stones so that the congregation might be overwhelmed with admiration. His aim was not only aesthetic brilliance and stylistic innovation, as many commentators have since maintained, but was also to enhance the possibility of a spiritual journey from the seen to the unseen world, *through* the visible to the invisible, *via* the material to the immaterial. It was to encourage the possibility that this spiritual journey would lead to a mystical experience, of being in a state of consciousness where the True Light of Christ is experienced as being "inherent in this world."[12]

If this really was Suger's intention, and there seems to me to be no reason to doubt it from his own writings, then another way of explaining the rise of the Gothic begins to open up to us.

For if his *primary* motivation for building in the New Style was neither architectural innovation nor aesthetic beauty, but a desire to house appropriately a certain type of mystical spirituality, then we must ask three questions: what precisely was that mystical spirituality, where did it come from and how exactly was the New Style an expression of, and an appropriate house for, it?

Bearing in mind all that has been put forward in the first chapter, there can only be one obvious direction in which answers to these questions can be found. This is in the mystical theology of Dionysius the Areopagite — with its origin in Syrian monasticism and its close affinity with Sufi mysticism, which the early Crusaders stumbled upon, and for which the Templars were enabled, with Sufi help, to find appropriate architectural form. This affinity was particularly marked in relation to the acceptance of God as hidden and unknown as much as revealed, and also that the divine darkness was as much part of mystical experience as divine light.

Exactly how these distinctive features of the New Style embodied the Dionysian-Sufi mysticism, will now be examined and, despite its detractors, it has to be said clearly that the vehicle of its embodiment had to have been sacred or symbolic geometry. For without geometry, ideas, archetypes and sacred concepts cannot be transformed into two-dimensional space. Likewise, it is only through geometry that two-dimensional drawings can be transformed into three-dimensional templates, and it is only through these templates that the work of the carpenter can be transferred to the mason. It is only in this way that the idea or concept can be transferred from the Divine Mind to the material world, and then transformed into built form. It was for this reason that geometry was considered to be the closest Liberal Art to the Divine Mind, and also why the stern injunction over the door of Plato's Academy in Athens said "Let no one who is not a geometer enter."[13] It was also for this reason that God himself was likened to a geometer and why in many medieval manuscripts he is pictured creating the world with a huge pair of compasses. All this had been known and practised for centuries by Muslim theologians, geometers and craftsmen, who were now becoming the agents of its transmission to western Europe. Laleh Bakhtiar speaks for the Sufi tradition in this regard: "The first two sciences to be explored are very close to the architectural art forms ... known as the sciences

Christ the Pantocrator: creating the world using compasses. French fourteenth-century manuscript.

Number	0	1	2	3	4	5	6
MACROCOSM	Divine Essence	**Creator**	**Intellect**	**Soul**	**Matter**	**Nature**	**Body**
		One Primordial Permanent Eternal	Innate Acquired	Vegetative Animal Rational	Original Physical Universal Artifacts	Ether Fire Air Water Earth	Above Below Front Back Right Left
Geometry							
Static		●	●—●				
Dynamic							
MICROCOSM	Divine Essence	**Creator**	**Body divided into two parts**	**Constitution of animals**	**Four humors**	**Five senses**	**Six powers of motion in six directions**
		One Primordial Permanent Eternal	Left Right	Two extremities and a middle	Phlegm Blood Yellow bile Black bile	Sight Hearing Touch Taste Smell	Up Down Front Back Left Right
MATHEMATICAL ATTRIBUTES		The point The principle and origin of all numbers	One-half of all numbers are counted by it	Harmony First odd number One-third of all numbers are counted by it	Stability First square number	First circular number	First complete number The number of surfaces in a cube

Sufi table of numerical and geometrical correspondences.

of numbers and geometry, the principles involved formed a basis for any further sciences."[14] Her table of Sufi numerical and geometrical correspondences is a succinct summary of the symbolic geometry which the Templars would have had to learn as a necessary prerequisite for becoming proficient in the arts and sciences of Islamic sacred architectural craftsmanship.

Chapter 3

ST BERNARD AND
THE EARLY GOTHIC PLAN

It would seem that, just as there was an initial gothic arch, the *mukhammas* or one-fifth Islamic arch, to which others were added later, so there was also an initial Gothic plan from which variations were later developed. In the absence of adequate documentation, this can be deduced by looking at the ground plans of four of the first Gothic cathedrals, namely Sens, Senlis, Paris and Chartres. It is possible, by measuring the crossings, to detect that they are all using the same proportional system, which points to a common source.

This common source is most likely to have been St Bernard, for three reasons: First, around 1130, it was Bernard who persuaded Henri de Sanglier, Archbishop of Sens, to rebuild his cathedral with this new plan, which was almost a decade *before* Suger began work on the pointed arches of his St Denis choir.[1] Second, Suger did *not* rebuild the nave of St Denis but worked first from the west and then from the east end, leaving the old nave untouched — supposedly because of a legend which said that Christ himself had built it, and that therefore it should not be changed.[2] Thus Sens, not St Denis, was the first complete Gothic ground plan to be set out and built. Third, in the sketch book of Villard de Honnecourt, there is a drawing of a typical ground plan for a Cistercian church which is clearly built to the same proportional system as that of Sens.[3] Bearing in mind that it was St Bernard who was head of the rapidly expanding Cistercian order, it can be deduced that he was the initiator and general disseminator of this standard plan, which was used, with minor differences, at Sens, the other early Gothic cathedrals listed above, and for at least some of the Cistercian monasteries.

Architectural historians have long accepted that St Bernard had a hands-on involvement with the development of Cistercian

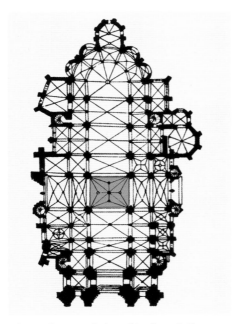

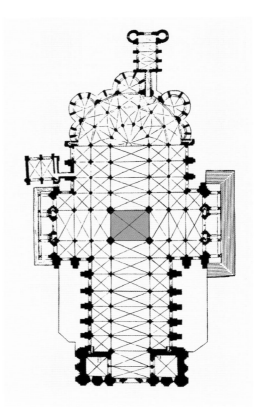

Above: The ground plan of Senlis and Chartres showing crossings of the same proportion.

Below: The ground plan of Sens and sketch of Cistercian plan by Villard de Honnecourt showing crossings of the same proportion.

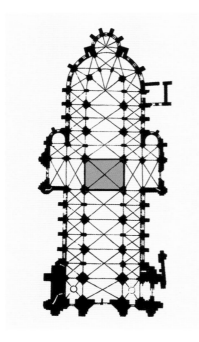

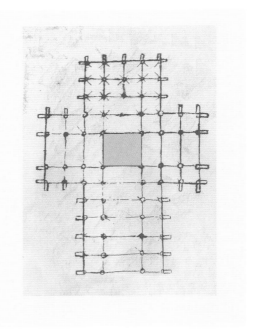

architecture, so much so that his contribution is called "the Bernardine Plan." Although its "precise characteristics and origins have been much debated," it is considered to have expanded and superceded earlier, simpler Cistercian plans in the mid-1130s, and to have probably been related to something like Villard de Honnecourt's Cistercian plan. The fact that Villard describes his plan as being for a square church, *vesci une glize desquarie*, could be a very good reason why scholars have not noticed that in fact it is not square, although Peter Ferguson has observed that the supposedly square crossings of certain Cistercian abbeys are actually rectangular. Ferguson's observation, the acknowledged importance of Villard and the mid-1130s dating of its first appearance of the Cistercian plans, all favour this interpretation of the Bernardine plan which I am putting forward.[4]

Even if St Bernard was only the disseminator and not the instigator of this common plan, the remarkable fact remains that, in essence, despite apparent differences, the plans of Sens, Senlis, Paris and Chartres are the same as each other and all are the same as Villard de Honnecourt's example of a typical Cistercian plan. This can be demonstrated by a close examination of their crossings, the central heart of the buildings where the horizontal line across the transepts crosses the vertical line of the nave and choir. This is most unexpected because commentators have usually stressed the difference between the anagogical theology of Suger and the austere puritanism of Bernard, between gaudy Gothic and simple Cistercian styles. Maybe they have been too quick to accept Lethaby's influential conclusion that: "It is vain to look, as many have done, for any general doctrines of proportion," or maybe they haven't bothered to apply ruler and compasses to the published plans.

Judging by more recent scholarship, it would seem that the latter is definitely the case, because, had a ruler been applied to the known plans, it would have been discovered that they are not quite as simple as they look. For instance, commenting on Villard de Honnecourt's Cistercian plan, Wim Swaan, in *The Gothic Cathedral*, is certain that it can easily be explained by analyzing its proportions as if they were the architectural equivalent to the ratios of musical intervals. It is natural that he should do so because this analogy with music had been the basis of Romanesque design, and indeed of most of the Classical tradition going back to the Romans and the Greeks. It was also considered to have been the system of proportions expressed in the ratios given by God to King David for the temple built by his son Solomon. In mainstream Christian tradition this musical analogy was begun by St Augustine who had taken it straight from Plato, as Plato had taken it from Pythagoras. As Wim Swaan says:

> St Augustine himself had placed music and architecture above the other arts, as being "sisters of number," and on occasion made much use of Pythagorean and Neo-Platonic number theory for his own purposes. The series 1:1, 1:2, 2:3, and 3:4 which correspond to the intervals of the perfect musical consonances: unison, octave, fifth and fourth, were heavily overlaid with Christian symbolism.[5]

In this, Swaan is accurately summarizing this ancient tradition in which sacred architecture was considered to be "frozen music," which originated in a Pythagorean interpretation of Solomon's Temple. He then goes on to apply this theory to Villard de Honnecourt's "simple" Cistercian plan. This must be quoted in full and then tested with a ruler on the actual plan (page 48).

> A simple and striking example of the application of the ratios of musical consonances to medieval architectural design, is afforded by the plan, from the sketch book of a thirteenth century architect-master-builder, of a Cistercian church with a square end and double square vaulting bays. The ratio of the fifth (2:3) determines the relationship of the width across the transepts to the total length; that of the octave (1:2) the relationship between the side aisle and the nave and also between the length and width of the transept; the musical fourth (3:4) is echoed by the proportion of the choir, while "the crossing," liturgically and aesthetically the centre of the church, is based on the 1:1 ratio of unison, most perfect of consonances.[6]

At first glance this analysis seems to be as accurate as it is predictable, for it follows the accepted musical symbolism of the Classical architectural tradition. But here it must be noted, we

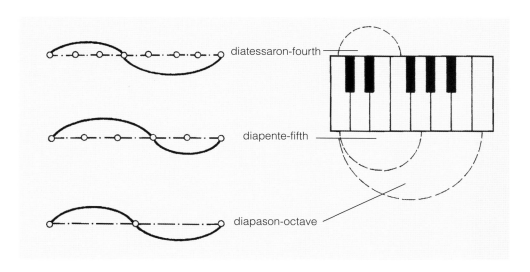

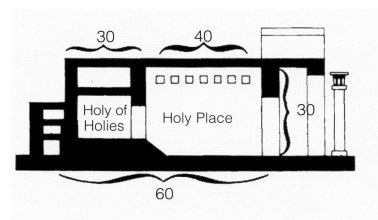

Top:
The proportions of the perfect musical intervals (number in time).

Bottom:
Solomon's Temple: The proportions of the perfect musical intervals transformed into architecture (number in space).

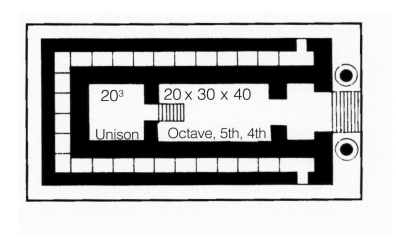

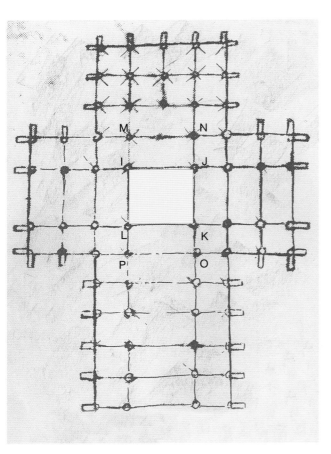

are dealing with the first flowering of the New Style which must surely have been different. Indeed, it might legitimately be asked: if this plan fits a Classical or Romanesque interpretation, how could it then have been new?

A contrast has often been made between Suger's visual and Bernard's essentially musical spirituality. On the basis of this and Bernard's apparent simple, austere aesthetic, it has been assumed that his Cistercian monasteries were all modelled on the simple ratios of Gregorian chant.[7] However, a close inspection of Villard de Honnecourt's Cistercian plan, shows this not to have been the case, at least in the instances cited.

The easiest way of deciding whether Wim Swaan is following the correct theory of architectural symbolism, is by checking the last of his assertions, that the crossing, that is the central meeting place of the horizontal transepts with the vertical nave-choir, is a square. He must think it is because only a square has the ratio of 1:1, which corresponds to the ratio of unison in music. If this proves to be correct, then all his other calculations must be correct because, by its very nature, the crossing defines all the other ratios in the building. If he is wrong, then it follows, all else is wrong.

The extraordinary thing is that even those with an untrained eye will have noticed that the crossing, marked *IJKL*, does not look very much like a square and, if it is measured, it reveals that *IJ* and *LK* are longer than *IL* and *JK*. One could object that this is only a sketch and that its accuracy, therefore, especially in a reproduction of a reproduction of an early medieval manuscript, cannot be relied on. Yet even with that caveat, it is possible to measure round the drawing and find the same discrepancy

Villard de Honne-court's sketch of a typical Cistercian plan. The crossing can be measured as 17 x 15 mm.

occurring regularly, which suggests that the analogy with music does not fit.

For instance, Wim Swaan claims that the vaulting is constructed in a series of double-bays forming the ratio 1:2, which is the musical equivalent of the octave. But is the double-bay *MNJI*, a double square? If it were, it would measure 16 mm by 8 mm, but in fact it measures 17 mm by 8 mm. Again it could be objected that this slight discrepancy can be explained away by the reasons given above. So if we concede this for the moment, let us go back and check the measurements of the "square" crossing. The longer sides *IJ* and *LK*, being the same as *MN*, are 17 mm, while the shorter sides *IL* and *JK* are found to be only 15 mm. So this is certainly *not* a square and I would contend, is *too much* not a square to be explained away by the age or sketchiness of the original drawing. Accurately measured, I believe that this marked discrepancy can be identified running throughout the whole plan; that the plan does not follow the symbolism of simple, whole number, musical ratios but that, like all Gothic plans, unlike anything before, it follows a symbolism based on geometry, not music. I make this assessment on the basis of calculating that the ratio between *IJ* and *JK* i.e. 17 mm and 15 mm, approximates very closely to half the ratio of one to the square root of three $(1:\sqrt{3}/2)$. Therefore, the rectangle formed by *MNOP*, being twice the size of the crossing, makes the ratio of its sides almost exactly one to the square root of three $(1:\sqrt{3})$. That this is so can be confirmed with a pocket calculator:

$$15 / 17 = 0.882$$
$$0.882 \times 2 = 1.764$$

The square root of three equals 1.732, so this small discrepancy of 0.032, since it is such a close approximation, can be taken as accurate. We shall find that the difference between 15 mm and 17 mm, on the plan, becomes nearly 245 cm (eight feet) when measured in real terms at Chartres.

In this way it is possible to demonstrate that Villard's Cistercian plan is not simple after all and does not follow the Romanesque or Classical symbolism of whole number ratios derived from music. It follows a pattern of ratios, which are based on the irrational fractions of geometry, not the whole number ratios of arithmetic. Geometric proportions are based on the use of compasses, whereas arithmetic proportions are based on the use of a ruler.

Here I believe that we have discovered the link between the built form of the new Gothic house of God and the particular spirituality, which it was designed to express. For when the Gothic designers changed from using the simple, whole number ratios of the Romanesque, to more complex ones like one to the square root of three — i.e. 1:1.732 — they were changing from ratios which could be exactly measured to those which could *not* be exactly measured and could only be drawn with compasses. In doing so they believed that they were coming closer to the Divine Mind and to God himself, the Great Architect of the Universe, because his chief characteristic was considered to be that he was ultimately immeasurable. In moving from *measurable* arithmetic to *immeasurable* geometry, they reflected a new desire to express the ultimate incomprehensibility of God. In other words, they had been gripped by the urge to express and embody a sense of the tremendous mystery of God's essential being. They could only do this by creating a sacred space in which none of the ratios could be measured precisely and could only be drawn with compasses. Understanding God as the Great Geometer therefore became the necessary pre-requisite for building churches which would be earthly reflections of this Divine mysteriousness.

As we have seen, the pointed arch, according to Sufi teaching, was considered to be more spiritual than the rounded arch because it moved from earth to air and on to heaven, and also because, being in the shape of the aura, was thought to be in tune with the subtle body. It was also regarded as spiritual because the ratio between its span and height never quite worked out in simple, whole numbers. For instance, the ratio between the span and height of the one-fifth arch should be exactly 5:3 but is not, because the centres of the two arcs, which make up the arch, are not exactly the same. Likewise in Villard's Cistercian plan, the same spirituality can be discerned in its use of the irrational, immeasurable geometric ratio of $1:\sqrt{3}$. This is a subtle but very important point, and constitutes the vital difference between Romanesque and Gothic. It also constitutes the difference between an architectural style, which housed a spirituality in which the mystical was present but marginal and subservient to the liturgy of the mass, and one in which it was central to the *raison d'être* of enhancing the possibility of mystical experience in the building itself, with or without the liturgy of the mass.

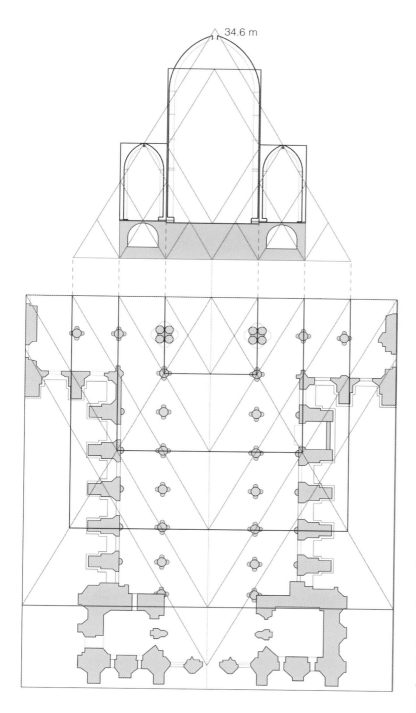

34.6 m

Cross section showing how main axes in the ground plan (which are defined by 1:√3 rectangles, see Chapter 6) are projected to bring geometry into the vertical dimension. The nave height is thus defined by a 1:√3 rectangle, as are the heights of the side aisles. The entire composition is defined by an equilateral triangle whose base length is also set by the geometry of the plan.

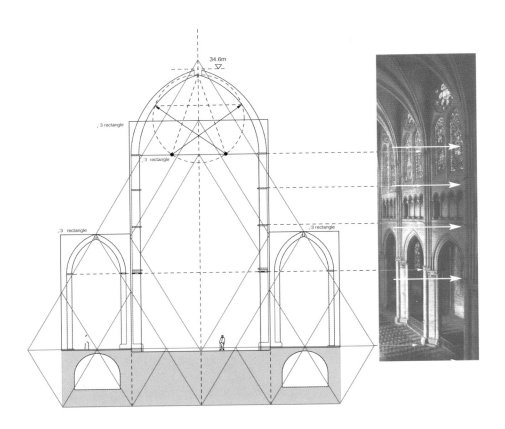

34.6m

√3 rectangle

√3 rectangle

√3 rectangle

√3 rectangle

Closer detail of the 1:√3 rectangles which define the width of the nave between the wall faces and also column faces. Note how the key dimensions of the main vault ribs are defined by a pentagram.

In all this we can understand more of what Suger meant by the anagogical journey from the material to the immaterial, but we can understand even more what Bernard meant when he said that, in architecture: "There must be no decoration, only proportion." This is because for him, the irrational, geometric proportions of the plan and by extension also the elevation, *in themselves*, — quite apart from the ornamentation so beloved by Suger — were the embodiment of a mystical theology closer to the heart of God than any style which had preceded it. For it explained God's ultimately immeasurable, incomprehensible mysteriousness and enhanced the possibility of experiencing the "beatific vision" which he, Bernard, believed was the goal of spirituality for all the faithful, and which he preached so eloquently.[8]

Chapter 4

OF CUBES AND KAABA

One of the most outrageous attacks on sacred geometry in recent years has come from Professor Eric Fernie of the Courtauld Institute in London, who believes that most of what has been written on the subject is quite simply sheer nonsense. He believes that it consists of "webs of literally unbelievable complexity and intellectual nullity." His invective is memorable:

> We are here in a sphere related to the almost pathological condition once described as pyramidiocy exemplified by the sad figure of Piazzi Smythe who, in the nineteenth century, visited Egypt as a respected Astronomer Royal and returned a convinced exponent of the biblical truths embedded in the layout of the Great Pyramid.[1]

This is based on the rhetorical trick of judging a great tradition, not by its best representatives such as some of the great Christian Platonists already mentioned, but by one of its most eccentric exponents. That apart, Professor Fernie's diatribe turns out to be empty rhetoric, not to say hot air, for he proves unable or unwilling to name a single example of twentieth century pyramidiocy. He also, and this is unforgivable in such a respected scholar, has failed to check the biblical reference he uses to justify his position. Wishing to take up the moral as well as the intellectual high ground, he quotes Ezekiel, but does so from the Ronald Knox translation, not realizing that Knox is now widely regarded as unreliable. The text is Ezekiel 43:10, which Knox translates as: "Who dares to measure the fabric of yonder Temple shall learn to blush for his misdeeds." Unfortunately for Eric Fernie, *all* the more recent, mainstream translators give *exactly the opposite* interpretation! For instance the Jerusalem Bible, New English Bible and the Revised Standard Version, all say that the prophet is describing the plan of the Temple to the

Internal elevation of South Transept and rose window.

sinful Israelites in order "to shame them out of their filthy practices." They will blush for their misdeeds when they see "the design and plan of the Temple." It is surprising that the Professor has allowed his prejudice to weaken his scholarship. Only a very charitable colleague could resist the temptation to be as scathing of him as he is of others.

Therefore, to continue charitably, it must be conceded that his outrageousness has led us to a most important question which comes directly from the biblical text, and is this: Why are the last nine chapters of Ezekiel full of the details of the measurements of the Temple? Why also, are the measurements of the Tabernacle of Moses given in such detail in Exodus? Likewise, the details of the measurements of Solomon's Temple in the First Book of the Kings and the Second Book of the Chronicles, and those of the New Jerusalem in Revelation 21? I believe that the answer to all these questions, tedious though it may seem to the likes of Eric Fernie and other sceptics mentioned in Chapter 2, is that for the Hebrews, as for all ancient cultures, the measurements defined ratios and proportions, which had to be exactly in tune with the harmony of heaven. As above, so below. This was the visual, harmonic and architectural equiv-alent of the ten commandments. As stated in the last chapter, the ratios of the architectural proportions had to be equivalent to the ratios of musical intervals which were considered to be the earthly echoes of the heavenly music of the spheres. Again, as stated, these were the ratios of 1:1, 1:2, 2:3 and 3:4, which were equivalent to unison, octave, fifth and fourth.

The distinction was also made strongly in the last chapter that, whereas this symbolism of musical intervals was used for Classical and Romanesque architecture, this was not the case for the Gothic. By contrast, it was explained, the Gothic changed to using geometric ratios, which were irrational fractions, because they wished to build churches, which would express God's ultimate mysteriousness and enhance the possibility of experiencing the Divine as the Great Mystery.

While this contrast still stands and is extremely important, it must now be modified to explain more precisely how the Gothic was *derived* from the Classical and did not exactly contrast with it. Strictly speaking the Gothic should not be contrasted with the Classical, but should be seen as complementary to, and as an advance upon it. To stay within the musical analogy it must now be stated that the square root ratios of geometry are *also* equivalent to musical intervals: $\sqrt{3}$ to the minor seventh and $\sqrt{2}$ to the tritone. Both of these are, in their own way, as important as the perfect intervals, though far more demanding and controversial. In fact, a more inclusive musical metaphor, and a possible cultural equivalent, could be made if Gothic geometrical ratios were likened to polyphony, which gradually developed from the simple, whole number ratios of "Romanesque" monody. How far this analogy can be taken it is not possible to explore at present, but the synchronicity between the musical and architectural developments from simplicity to complexity in the twelfth and thirteenth century, is very striking.

The way in which this complex musical metaphor can be explained in terms of its equivalent geometry is by examining two different ways of understanding the same geometric figure. This figure is not two- but three-dimensional. It must be borne in mind that the transformation of geometry into architecture involves moving from two- to three-dimensional space. Thus taking the musical ratio of unison — i.e. 1:1 — which geometrically is a square and transforming it into its architectural equivalent, makes it into the ratio 1:1:1, which is a cube.

Now it is a musical, acoustic fact of the physics of vibration that when the full string length of any musical instrument, such as a guitar or violin, is plucked, the vibrating string sounds a note — called the tonic — and also, very faintly, sounds all the other notes, which are contained within it such as the octave, fifth, fourth, etc. These are so faint that they can only be heard by those with *very* acute hearing. They are called the harmonic overtones and when they are picked out on the shaft of a guitar for instance, they become the frets.

Ancient cultures studied these harmonic overtones in detail

and were fascinated by the discovery that they were always there, vibrating faintly whenever the full string length was plucked. Furthermore, they were so impressed by the realization that the full string length contained, however faintly, all the other notes of music, that for them unison was the most important note; unison singing was the most important form of singing, and the ratio 1:1 was the most important ratio. In geometrical terms this was equivalent to the square, and in architecture the cube.

It is necessary to explain all this clearly because it is otherwise impossible for us today to comprehend why in Solomon's Temple, the Holy of Holies (the innermost sacred sanctuary, which housed the Ark of the Covenant and the cherubim), was in the shape of a cube. It is also impossible to understand why Yahweh was said to speak to his people from above the ark and between the wings of the cherubim, unless we realize that this was at the quincunx, or dead centre, of the cube, which vibrationally was the place of power and transformation, just as it is within any pyramid shape.

It is also otherwise incomprehensible that the shape of the New Jerusalem in the New Testament should also be a cube. Most illustrations of the New Jerusalem over the centuries have taken no notice of this despite the fact that it states explicitly in Revelation 21: "its length and breadth and height are equal."

The primary importance of the cube and the musical-vibrational symbolism it represented, was not restricted to the Judeo-Christian tradition. It can also be found in the east in Hindu temples and, most significantly for this enquiry, in traditional Muslim mosques.

In Islamic architecture the cube is not only the primary structure at the centre of the mosque, over which an octagon leads up to the circular dome; it is also, and this is the really important factor, the primary geometric figure from which many of the Islamic patterns, which are such distinctive features of Islamic art and architecture, are derived and formed.

How can this be? How can geometry be derived from the arithmetical ratios 1:1:1? How can square root ratios emerge from such an elementary, simple figure as the cube? The answer is very straight forward: By means of the two ratios which are implicit in the cube, which are not simple but which were regarded in Islamic architectural theory as being as integral to the cube as the simple ratios 1:1:1. These implicit ratios were

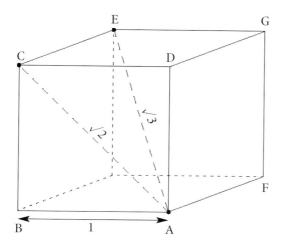

firstly, the sides of the square faces of the cube in relation to their diagonals which were always the ratio of one to the square root of two (1:$\sqrt{2}$) and second, the diagonal of the cube itself which was one to the square root of three (1:$\sqrt{3}$). These measurements can be proved by the theorem of Pythagoras which states that in any right-angled triangle, the square of the hypotenuse is equal to the sum of the squares of the other two sides.

Owing to Islam's strict adherence to the Old Testament prohibition against creating images, its equally strict positive acceptance of the detail of the proportions of Solomon's and Ezekiel's Temples, and also its encouragement of learning as *akbar jahd* (the greatest effort), Islam had absorbed Euclid's geometry and fused it with the best of traditional Persian art to create a new abstract visual language with which to express the truths of the Koran in appropriate art and architecture. The architectural starting place for all that they went on to achieve in this creative synthesis, was the ancient shrine at Mecca which was supposed to have been built by Adam, rebuilt by Abraham and his son, Ishmael, cleansed of idols and re-dedicated to Allah by Muhammad. This shrine was and is called the Kaaba, which means Cube, because it is in the form of a cube.[2] It is this cube, the Kaaba, which is more important to the rise of the Gothic style, than the cube of the Holy of Holies of Solomon's Temple or the cube of the New Jerusalem. Both of these other biblical cubes were important because both Solomon's Temple and the New Jerusalem are often quoted as

Cube showing $\sqrt{2}$ diagonal of a square face and $\sqrt{3}$ diagonal of the cube itself.

The Kaaba at Mecca.

models in Gothic sources. However, the Kaaba was more important because it was from the cube of the Kaaba that the architecture, based on its inherent $\sqrt{2}$ and $\sqrt{3}$ ratios, was derived. An examination of the basic structure of Islamic patterns in art and architecture demonstrates this point.[3]

I believe it was this *geometric* as distinct from *arithmetic*, architectural tradition which the first Crusaders discovered and about which the Templars learned enough to transfer to northern France. I believe they saw excellent examples of it in Jerusalem and especially on the Temple Mount. For while I believe their model for the one-fifth arch came from the Aksa Mosque as explained in Chapter 1, I believe their model for building to ratios of $1:\sqrt{2}$ and $1:\sqrt{3}$ came from the other even more magnificent building on the Temple Mount, the Dome of the Rock, already described. If the elevation of this great shrine is analysed geometrically, it will be found that the two outer circular ambulatories form the ratios of $\sqrt{2}$ and $\sqrt{3}$ additions to the central square of the building.[4]

I believe it is no coincidence that, of the early cathedrals built in the New Gothic Style, one — Laon — was built on the ratio between the side and the diagonal of the square, i.e. $1:\sqrt{2}$ and that the other four — Sens, Senlis, Paris and Chartres — were built on the ratio between the side and the diagonal of the cube, i.e. 1:$\sqrt{2}$. In the technical Latin phraseology of the medieval masons the first of these, the 1:$\sqrt{2}$ system, was known as *ad quadratum,* meaning it was built "to the square," and the second, the 1:$\sqrt{3}$, was known as *ad triangulum*, because it was built "to the triangle." The particular triangle referred to was the equilateral triangle in which all three sides are equal.[5]

How this triangle is related to the square root of three and how it applies to the plan of Chartres, and indeed also applies to the plan of Sens, Senlis, Paris and the Cistercian plan of Villard de Honnecourt, must now be explained. For while it is easy to understand how building "to the square" would naturally produce square buildings, it is not so easy to understand why building "to the triangle" did *not* produce triangular buildings!

Cross section of the Dome of the Rock showing $\sqrt{2} + \sqrt{3}$ proportions.

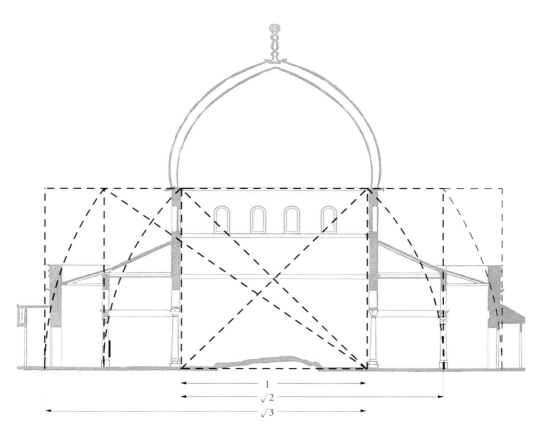

$$1$$
$$\sqrt{2}$$
$$\sqrt{3}$$

Chapter 5

THE PLAN OF CHARTRES

In the traditional understanding of the three monotheistic religions of Judaism, Christianity and Islam, the only way in which it was believed the Oneness of God could be expressed architecturally was by the means of the cube. The cube alone expressed the perfection of Oneness because it alone had the ratios of 1:1:1. This is another way of explaining the supreme importance of the cube of the Holy of Holies of Solomon's Temple, the New Jerusalem and the Kaaba, as described.

As we have seen, it was only the Islamic geometers and masons who worked out how the ratios of one to the square root of two and one to the square root of three — inherent in the diagonal of the square faces and the diagonal of the whole cube — could be developed into systems of architectural proportion. We have also seen how, when these were appropriated by the Crusaders for the Christian West, they became known as *ad quadratum*, building "to the square" and its diagonal of $\sqrt{2}$ and *ad triangulum*, building "to the cube" and its diagonal of $\sqrt{3}$.

It is extraordinary that in addition to this, the simple cube provided the basis for *yet another* tradition of architecture and architectural symbolism, which, while overlapping considerably with the Islamic, may have been originally Christian from very early times. The knowledge of it may have been preserved and honoured by the Sufis, and it may well be that it was from the Sufis that the Templars rediscovered it, but it is doubtful whether it was ever used in Islam as such, however similar the two traditions were.

This other and probably uniquely Christian way of using the cube as the basis of an architectural system with its attendant symbolism, was based on looking at it axonometrically (at an angle of 45°). It may seem far-fetched and strange, but if you look at a cube in this way you will find that it turns into a hexagon. A hexagon is a six-sided figure with all its sides equal. The

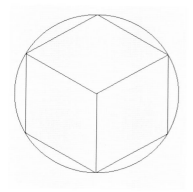

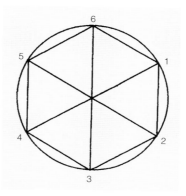

cube, in three dimensions, is still a cube but at this angle it turns into, or appears to be, a two-dimensional hexagon. So it is a cube *and* a hexagon at the same time. It is in fact a cube-as-hexagon. A hexagon is made up of six equilateral triangles, and it was these which formed the basis of the main proportional system used in the early Gothic, known as *ad triangulum*. For although the knowledge and technical skills needed to build it came from Islam, the particular variation or "spin," which the Gothic builders gave it, seems not to have been Islamic but to have derived from a much earlier, forgotten branch of the Christian Church. Where exactly it came from perhaps we will never know but Frederick Bligh Bond, whose researches in the early nineteenth century, led to the rediscovery of it, was convinced it came from Christian Gnostic sources, particularly a document called the *Pistis Sophia* and also the *Books of Ieou*. He also believed that the rediscovery of this Gnostic tradition took place during the twelfth century, and that it led directly to the rise of the Gothic style.[1]

I believe Bligh Bond's theory to be correct, and that it has been confirmed by John James' rigorous architectural analysis of Chartres in his two definitive books, *The Contractors of Chartres* and *The Master Masons of Chartres*. A thorough reading of these masterpieces leaves sceptics little justification for their prejudice.

John James believed that there were teams of masons who built Chartres, and he lists, perhaps significantly, nine in all who, as it were, worked shifts over the twenty-five years between 1194, when it was started, and 1220, when it was all but finished. Without going into the complexities of the different units of measurement which were used by these teams of

Left:
Axonometric view of a cube which forms a hexagon in two dimensions.

Right:
The cube as hexagon composed of six equilateral triangles.

masons, it is sufficient to say that he came to the conclusion that, at Chartres, it was the Roman Foot (RF) which was used as the basic unit. He came to this conclusion because, if he measured the Cathedral in Roman Feet, its ratios and proportions worked out in whole numbers, whereas if he used the English foot, metres, cubits or any other unit, they did not. The Roman Foot is only fractionally shorter than the English Imperial foot, for seven of them — which made up one Greek Fathom, another ancient measure — add up to 6.8 English feet. So one Roman Foot was 0.97143 of an English foot.

John James' diagram of the crossing at Chartres. This fractional difference, he realized, was important because he found that the crossing, already mentioned in Chapter 2, measured 56 RF exactly across the nave from the centre of one pier to the centre of the other, and 48 RF across

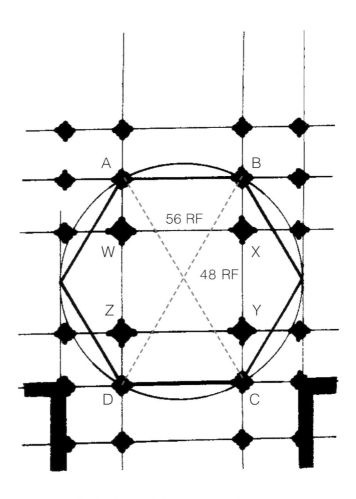

the transepts from centre pier to centre pier. This was an exciting discovery because the ratio between 56 and 48 is 7 to 6:

$$8 \times 7 = 56 \text{ and } 8 \times 6 = 48.$$

Here we must once again remember how important ratios and proportions were in traditional sacred architecture, and also how important the symbolism of numbers was which went together with them. John James is no stranger to the symbolism of numbers or geometry and on the basis of his wide knowledge, he confidently asserts that seven is the number of the Virgin Mary, six is the number of the perfect man, Jesus, and that the place where the two axes meet at the crossing, symbolizes, in architectural space, the same as that which is sculptured over the south door of the West Portal — namely Mary as Wisdom and Jesus as Logos.[2]

I believe that John James is correct in this interpretation because seven, unlike nine, being an indivisible prime number which has no factors, was likened to a virgin who had no children and six, being a rare "perfect" number, i.e. one which was the sum of its divisors, was ideal for Jesus. However, I also believe that, in his diagram of the layout of the crossing, he has made an even more important discovery which, on close inspection, confirms all that was put forward in Chapter 2, regarding the crossing of Villard de Honnecourt's Cistercian plan.

A hexagon can be drawn inside a circle by dividing its circumference into six equal parts. All hexagons drawn within circles have six equal sides, each of which is equal to the radius of the circle. This means that it can be divided into six equilateral triangles. As you can see in John James' diagram, this is the simple geometry which explains the crossing at Chartres.[3]

The circle which contains the hexagon passes through the nave columns at points D and C and through the Choir columns at A and B. DC and AB coincide exactly with the axes of these columns. If we now look at the rectangle $ABCD$, we can work out the length of AD and BC by the theorem of Pythagoras for, as just said, AB and DC equal the radius and therefore AC and BD, being equal to the diameter, will be twice the radius. In any right angled triangle, the square on the hypotenuse is equal to the sum of the squares on the other two sides. It follows that in triangle ADC, $AD^2 + DC^2 = AC^2$. As $AC = 2$ and $DC = 1$ it follows that $AD = \sqrt{3}$. So, if DC and AB are 1 then AD and BC are $\sqrt{3}$. The rectangle $ABCD$ is therefore what is called a root three

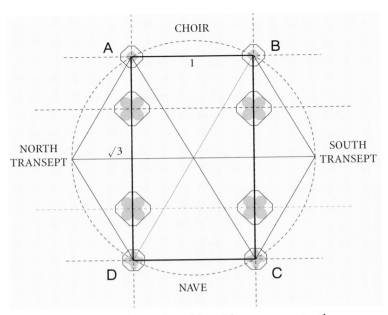

NAVE

The main 1:$\sqrt{3}$ rectangle defined by the crossing forming the basic unit of the ad triangulum geometry in plan.

rectangle because the ratio of its sides are one to the square root of three (1:$\sqrt{3}$).

This $\sqrt{3}$ rectangle is twice the size of the crossing *WXYZ*. John James measured this, and found that the ratio between its longer and shorter sides is 56:48 or 7:6 (we have verified these dimensions on site). Seven to six is the ratio of half a $\sqrt{3}$ rectangle, for:

$$7 \times \sqrt{3}/2 = 6$$

Well not precisely. It is precisely 6.062, which is very close. Closer than the ratio between 17 and 15 mm, as measured on the crossing on Villard de Honnecourt's Cistercian plan, which when multiplied by two, came to 1.764, or only 0.032 more than $\sqrt{3}$, which is 1.732.

This illustrates the paradox implicit in the whole debate that a $\sqrt{3}$ rectangle can be precisely drawn with compasses, but not precisely measured.

In this way it is simple to demonstrate how the six equilateral triangles which make up a hexagon, form the geometrical frame for the 1:$\sqrt{3}$ rectangle, which is the basic unit of the *ad triangulum* system of building (see figure above and right).

The way in which the geometry of the crossing defines the general shape of the cathedral, can be discovered by extending the longer sides *AC* and *BD*. It is found that they coincide with the lines of columns on each complete side of the nave to the west and the full length of the choir to the east. Furthermore, if the shorter sides *AB* and *CD* are extended, it is found that they define the transept walls to the north and the south (see below).

Further confirmation of the accuracy of this geometry at Chartres can be demonstrated by drawing another, smaller circle inside the √3 rectangle *ABCD*. This circle will have a radius of 28 RF, which is half the bigger one. If another hexagon is drawn inside this smaller circle, it will be found that it not only defines the line of all the columns across the transepts but that, by joining all the diagonals of this geometry, the positions of *all* the columns in the *whole building* are defined.

In other words, this simple geometrical figure of a hexagon inside a hexagon at the crossing, when extended out in all directions (see page 66), proves to be the key to the layout and pattern of the whole cathedral!

What Lethaby called a vain quest for an overall theory of Gothic design — what Morgan scorned and Fernie derided — is not so vain, adventitious or lunatic after all. John James must be congratulated for discovering the key to this sacred pattern,

A lattice of diagonals emerge from the central 1:√3 rectangle to define the position of all the columns in the plan.

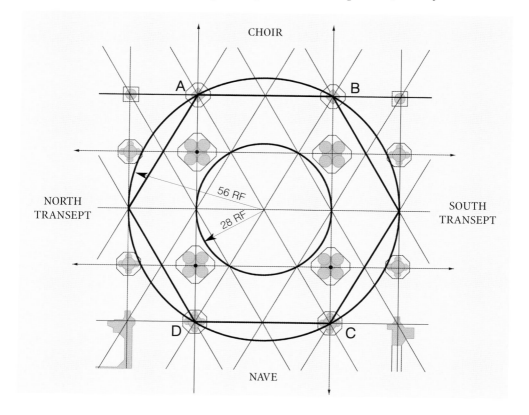

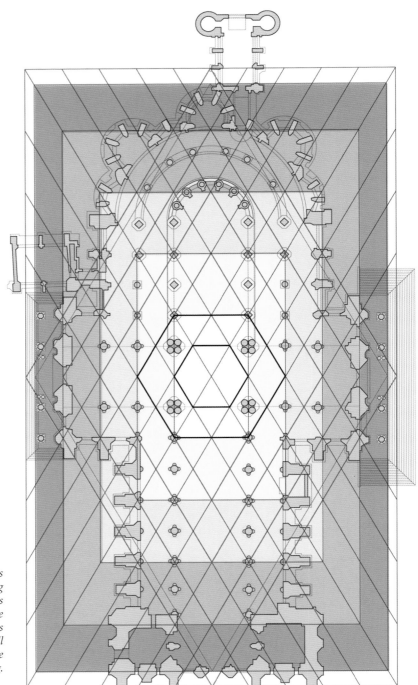

Plan of Chartres cathedral showing how diagonals drawn from the central hexagons locate almost all the columns in the building.

which can be applied with equal success to the plans of Sens, Senlis, Laon and Villard de Honnecourt's Cistercian church. This *is* a general theory of proportions and it fits precisely. Why wasn't it discovered before? Perhaps because no one, before John James, had combined professional architectural expertise, and painstaking on-site scrutiny, with a mind-set in tune with the Christian Platonism of the medieval masons. Perhaps also because no one had fully realized that the unit, the module used throughout, was not a single bay, but a double bay. It is only when that point is grasped that the lattice of diagonals, which defines all the columns, becomes clear. This lattice is itself made up of numerous equilateral triangles in units of two, lying base to base and forming what are called *rhombuses.* The ratio between the width and the length of each of these rhombuses is $1:\sqrt{3}$, thus showing that the *ad triangulum* principle, like a hologram, runs throughout all the individual sub-units which together make up the cathedral building.

All that has been said above fits in well with the theory that Gothic architecture based on the *ad triangulum* ratio of 1 to $\sqrt{3}$, was brought to north-west Europe first by captured Islamic masons, and later by Templars and probably other Crusaders, who had learnt it from the Muslims in general and Sufis in particular. If this is so, then why was it necessary to put forward the hypothesis that this Islamic tradition was given a Christian "spin," based on the cube-as-hexagon, which was derived from ancient Christian Gnostic sources? Surely the main point of changing from simple arithmetical architectural ratios based on whole number musical intervals, to irrational geometric square root ratios, was to express a desire to build churches appropriate for a more mystical theology in which the striking similarities between Sufi wisdom and the mysticism of Dionysius the Areopagite (St Denis) were outlined. This is indeed the case and there is no intention of minimizing the overwhelming Islamic influence. Yet that does not exclude the possibility that a similar and earlier Christian source, later rejected or forgotten by the western Church but preserved by the Sufis, could have been shown by the Sufis to the Templars and been used by them to develop a specifically Christian edition of the Islamic tradition. There has been so much architectural borrowing between the different religions over the centuries, that I believe this to be a distinct possibility.

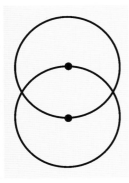

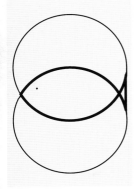

But the reason for suggesting the possibility of this earlier Gnostic influence is primarily because within the Christian tradition, the *ad triangulum* system of building was closely associated not only with the equilateral triangle and the cube-as-hexagon but also with a geometric construction which was constantly used as a specifically Christian symbol and never to my knowledge as an Islamic one. This geometric figure came from the Greeks and, like the Greek theory of architecture as "frozen music," was commandeered for the purposes of Christian symbolism without any changes being made. It was quite simply two circles whose circumferences passed through each other's centres. In the Greek world it represented the number two (the Dyad) becoming three (the Triad), and was called the *Potential Logos*. When the Christians took it over, it became known as the *vesica piscis,* the womb, or bladder, of the fish. The fish was Jesus Christ who was the Word Incarnate, the New Logos, the Mediator between heaven and earth and whose title, Fish in Greek, spelt ICHTHUS, the mnemonic for the first creed: **I**esous (Jesus) **Ch**ristos (Christ) **Th**eou (of God) **U**ios (son) **S**oter (Saviour).[4]

This symbol may well have come from the Gnostics because it has often been noted that there is much Pythagoreanism and Platonism mixed into Gnostic texts, and it was used by both Pythagoras and Plato. For Plato the three elements of the Potential Logos were called the *Same* and the *Other* with *Essence* in the middle. For Pythagoras these were called the *Limited* and the *Unlimited* held together by *Logos*. Either way, it is definitely Greek in origin and it is obvious how easily it could be used to fit a Christian interpretation.[5]

It is similar to the eastern Yin and Yang symbol since the polarities — of Same and Other, and Limited and Unlimited — represent the Masculine and Feminine principles, which run through creation. However, unlike the Yin-Yang polarity, there is a third element, the central overlap, representing that

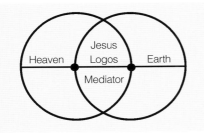

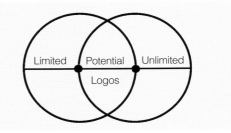

which is born out of the balance of opposites. This is important because it takes the figure of Jesus beyond gender, and Mary too, who as Ever Virgin must also be regarded as an androgynous symbol. In fact, although it is not possible to examine this dimension here in any detail, this element of divine androgyny leads on to astrology.

Mary, as Ever Virgin, is symbolic of the zodiacal house of Virgo and Jesus her son "born of the Virgin Mary," is the Fish, which is the zodiacal house of Pisces. Virgo and Pisces are opposite and complementary houses and form one of the six axes in the circle of the zodiac. Most importantly, they are the joint rulers of the Age of Pisces, the period of 2,160 years, which began with the birth of Christ. Strictly speaking, in astrological terms, each sign comes with its opposite, complementary sign. Thus the Age of Pisces should really be called the Age of Pisces-Virgo. It can be inferred that, consciously or unconsciously, the early and medieval Church knew this by the use of the credal mnemonic ICHTHUS, and by the pervasive use of astrological symbolism in the iconography of the Gothic cathedrals.[6] This

Pisces (top right) and Aquarius (centre) on the zodiac window.

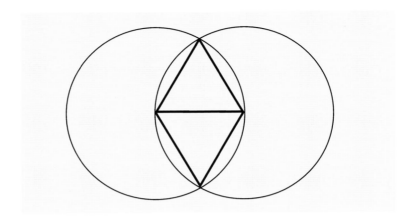

Rhombus in a vesica, made up of two equilateral triangles.

can be seen at Chartres by the presence of the zodiacal sculptures round the arch above the north door of the Western Portal, and also by the zodiac window in the south aisle of the choir. It can also be inferred by the fact that the main sculptured image above the great central door of the Western Portal shows a huge Christ inside a huge *vesica piscis*, while on the *inside* of the western front, at the top of the central window under the rose, there is a stained glass image of the Virgin Mary picked out in blue and red, inside a large *vesica piscis*.

The image of Christ as the mediator and Great Fish, within the *vesica piscis* is so commonly seen carved over the west door of late Romanesque and early Gothic churches, that it is difficult to entertain the likelihood of an Islamic connection. Yet there is a strong link between the $1:\sqrt{3}$ ratio, as derived from the cube and the *vesica piscis*. There is also a very close connection between the equilateral triangle and the *vesica piscis* which can be simply demonstrated.

As described above, the easiest way of constructing a hexagon is by dividing the circumference of a circle into six equal parts, each the same length as the radius. This can then be divided into six equilateral triangles. If a second circle is drawn so that its circumference passes through the centre of the first, then a *vesica piscis* is formed, into which two of the six equilateral triangles fit exactly. These two equilateral triangles, which lie base to base, form a rhombus, which is the same as the rhombuses formed by the lattice of diagonals when the Chartres plan, based on John James' hexagon, was analysed above. Then we examined the *ad triangulum* $1:\sqrt{3}$ ratio from the crossing outwards to the rest of the building. Now we find

Opposite: The famous sculpture in the West Portal showing the direct link between Christ and the cathedral plan as described.

CHARTRES: SACRED GEOMETRY, SACRED SPACE

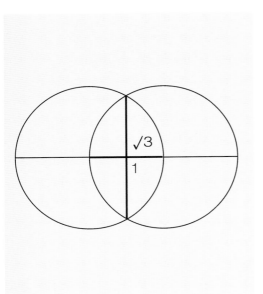

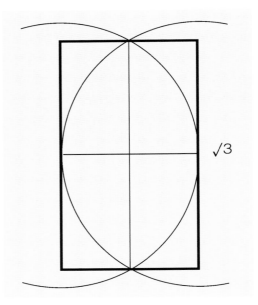

that the rhombus inside the vesica defines the *ad triangulum* proportional system from the outside inwards.

As mentioned above, the ratio between the width and length of any rhombus is 1:√3. If, therefore, we want to construct a Gothic *ad triangulum* plan from the outside inwards, we must construct a rectangle which encloses the *vesica piscis*. This will have sides of ratio 1:√3. This 1:√3 rectangle contains within it the *vesica piscis* and the rhombus. From this it is possible to create a series of smaller 1:√3 rectangles and vesicas which will eventually bring us back to the smallest 1:√3 rectangle, which we identified and analysed at the crossing with John James.

So, either from the central crossing by means of the hexagon, or from the outer shell of the *vesica piscis*, the same pattern emerges. This is the basic pattern of early Gothic, which ultimately would appear to be as Christian as it is Islamic. Maybe this is something for our Islamophobic western world to ponder. For without the genius of Islam, it is doubtful if there would ever have been any Gothic cathedrals. Without the Sufis, how could the Templars have learnt about the universality and ultimate oneness of truth? Yet without the militant, if misguided, zeal of the Crusaders, how would they have ever rediscovered and entered into their own lost Gnostic heritage?

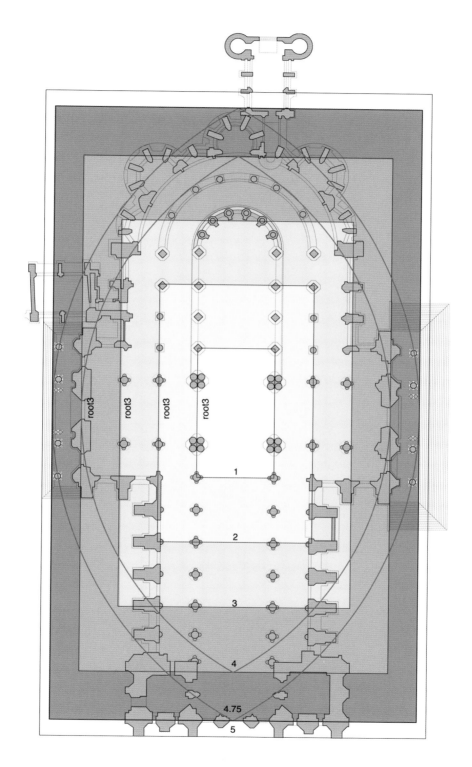

Chapter 6

DIONYSIUS THE AREOPAGITE AND THE UNKNOWN GOD

In the last chapter the general assertion that the Gothic style came from Islam via the Sufis and the Templars, had to be qualified by the assertion that the Christian "spin" on this probably came from earlier lost Gnostic sources, such as the *Pistis Sophia* and the *Book of Ieou*. This in turn must now be qualified as, strictly speaking, it would appear to have come not from Gnostic sources, which are usually considered to be second or third century, but from even earlier, from the first century — from Dionysius the Areopagite (St Denis) himself and Clement I, third Bishop of Rome.

As explained in earlier chapters, the transmission of Sufi ideas back to France in the twelfth century, via the Templars, was made possible because of the remarkable similarities which were discovered between the Sufi inclusive spirituality and the mystical theology of Dionysius the Areopagite. This was instanced by the importance of the symbolism of the number nine to both these traditions, and also to that of the early Templars, who were reputed to have only been nine in number for their first nine years. It has also been stated earlier that this Dionysius had had his name contracted to Denis, or Denys, and that as St Denis he later became the first bishop and patron saint of Paris and of the Abbey, from which Abbot Suger launched his New Style in 1144.

St Denis, the third-century martyred Bishop of Paris.

The story of Dionysius the Areopagite, otherwise known as St Denis, is very complex because, not only is he often confused with the martyred third-century bishop of Paris, but also with a late fifth-century Syrian monk, who actually wrote mystical theology under that assumed name, and is thus known as "Pseudo-Dionysius." So, in all, like the Holy Trinity, there were three Dionysiuses who were collated by tradition into one composite character.[1]

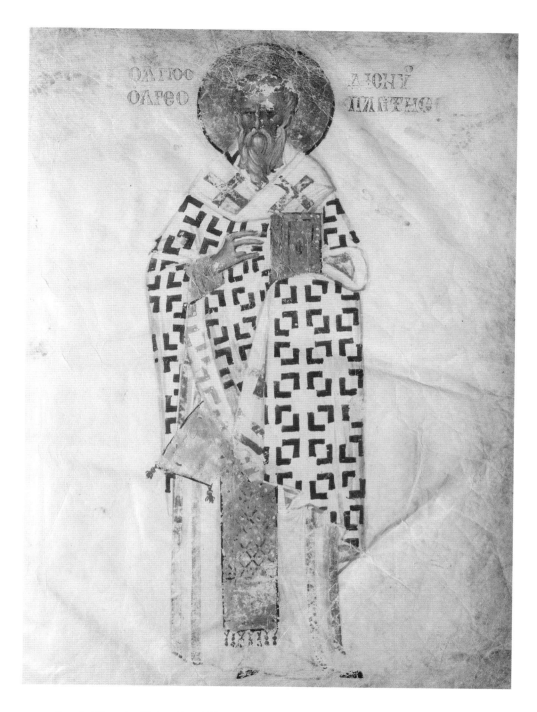

Pseudo-Dionysius (St Denis), a fifth-century Syrian monk, author of The Mystical Theology.

It is the first of these who is the most important because, as mentioned earlier, the inception of a school of Christian Platonism was attributed to him, which arose as a result of his conversion in Athens by St Paul. He was called "the Areopagite," which literally means "the field of Aries or Mars," because this was where the Senate of the city met, and he was a senator of the city. Tradition tells us that he was actually the president. He was therefore a high-ranking civic dignitary and so would have been in a position to influence others. He was obviously considered to have become an equally important Christian because later biographers say he was either Bishop of Athens or of Corinth. That he was also thought to have been the third-century Bishop of Paris and the fifth-century Syrian mystical theologian, testifies more to the strength of the tradition he started than to the dubious historical credentials of his hagiographers! His name was given to, or taken by, those who later carried on his tradition of Christian Platonism.[2]

Before we move on to later centuries, it is important to examine a certain aspect of the story of St Paul's famous address to the Athenian senate, as it is found in Acts 17. Paul

St Paul's famous address to the Athenian senate (cartoon for the Sistine Chapel) by Raphael. Dionysius the Areopagite and Danaris are pictured bottom right.

CHARTRES: SACRED GEOMETRY, SACRED SPACE

had been preaching against idols in the Jewish synagogue and was then apprehended by some Epicurean and Stoic philosophers who dragged him off to the Areopagus, to give an account of his beliefs to the city fathers. Unlike in other sermons, Paul took a reasonable rather than a dogmatic approach. Instead of continuing to criticize their idolatry, he quickly changed to flattery, congratulating them on being very religious and for having an altar dedicated "to an unknown god" in addition to all their statues of sundry divinities. His punchline was, of course, that Jesus was the Christ revealed by God: "What therefore you worship as unknown, this I proclaim to you." (Acts 17:23).

In the Greek text of the New Testament "TO AN UNKNOWN GOD" is written in capitals as AGNOSTO THEO — to the *not-known* God. At first sight, this only appears to be a master stroke of rhetoric which held his audience, even if, by the time he had finished, most mocked him and only Dionysius, a woman called Damaris and a few others were converted. However, there is another, more subtle point which can be taken from this, which relates to the tradition of mystical theology, said to have derived from this momentous occasion. The mystical theology of Dionysius the Areopagite — which few would doubt was actually written by the fifth-century Syrian monk of the same name — has, as one of its most important distinguishing features, the concept of the "unknown" God. God the Unknown, despite having been revealed in Jesus Christ, is still ultimately unknown and unknowable. The similarity between the AGNOSTO THEO theme in the story of Paul's conversion of Dionysius on Mars Hill, and the concept of the Unknown God in the fifth-century writings of Pseudo-Dionysius, is so striking that it is difficult not to believe in the authenticity of this theme from the first-century Dionysius to the fifth-century Dionysius.

In this typical excerpt, Pseudo-Dionysius is making the point which he repeats again and again, that because of our finite minds we cannot comprehend the infinite; because of our limited language, we cannot describe the unlimited; and because even our symbols only partake a fraction of that which they symbolize, they must in the end be abandoned as inadequate. Even to call God Father or Son or Holy Spirit, or any other name, becomes an obstacle to grasping his transcendence. This is the way of *unknowing*, of ignorance, which cannot be described:

It cannot be grasped by the understanding since it is neither knowledge nor truth. It is not kingship. It is not wisdom. It is neither one nor oneness, divinity or goodness. Nor is it a spirit, in the sense in which we understand that term. It is not sonship nor fatherhood and it is nothing known to us or to any other being. It falls neither within the predicate of nonbeing nor of being. Existing beings do not know it as it actually is and it does not know them as they are. There is no speaking of it, nor name or knowledge of it.[3]

This is the language of paradox which lies at the heart of much Christian mysticism. The paradox: "It falls neither within the predicate of non-being nor of being," is typical of later mystical writings such as *The Cloud of Unknowing,* and, being part of a more sophisticated spirituality, is not usually thought to have originated at an early date. Therefore, the late fifth-century date for Pseudo-Dionysius suits very well.

However, there are grounds for believing that such mystical language of paradox was in evidence as early as the first century. This comes from the Seventeenth Homily of Clement I, the third Bishop of Rome who, as St Peter's successor, claimed to be speaking for him when he was supposedly challenged to name the place where God lived by the Gnostic heretic, Simon Magus, His answer is very Dionysian, which is most intriguing, because the earliest sources for the legendary life of Dionysius say that he went to Rome and worked with Clement I, and together they planned a mission to the pagans in Gaul.[4]

Since this mission took place in the third century, this part of the story cannot be treated as historical. Yet there is no doubting the connection between the Areopagite and the third Bishop of Rome, with regard to the sophisticated knowledge of the language of mystical paradox. St Peter said:

But someone will say: "If God has Form, He also has Fashion and is in a Place, but if in a place, then He must be smaller than the place which contains Him, and how can He then be great above all things? And how can He be everywhere being of a Fashion?"

But first I will speak of Place, and the Place of God is "That-which-is-not," but God is "That-which-is." But "that-which-is-not" is not comparable with "That-which-is." For how can that which is a place be said to exist unless there be a second region, such as Heaven, earth, water, air or any other such body, which can occupy the space to hold it, which for that very fact is called empty because it is nothing. For this, "The no-thing" is its more suitable designation.[5]

However unintelligible this passage may be to those un-familiar with the language of paradox, it is not hard to see the similarity between this and Dionysius, for the paradox expressed by Clement, between the Place of God being "That-which-is-not" *and* "That-which-is," is very similar to the Dionysian paradox between Him being neither "non being nor of being". This is surprising because it implies that sophisti-cated mystical language was being used in the Age of the first Apostles, and that St Peter was more of a profound philosopher than a simple fisherman by the time he got to Rome!

To return to the tradition which claims that Dionysius came to Rome, worked with this same Clement, and planned his mission to Gaul with him — although the latter claim must be historically discounted — the similarity between them in their use of the language of paradox, would appear to validate the former. It could even perhaps be claimed that the Are-opagite taught Clement the use of paradox from his own Greek, philosophical background. Whatever the precise rela-tionship, it is clear that, in the first century, it is possible to trace the development of this strand of Christian mysticism directly from Athens to Rome. What is even more unexpected is that however unhistorical the Dionysian lineage appears to be, from the point of view of today's strict standard of historicity, there is evidence to show that this same lineage somehow came to Paris, that it was associated with the third-century Dionysius, otherwise called St Denis, and that it was known to Abbot Suger,[6] St Bernard[7] and the other initiators of the New Style.

This evidence comes from the same Seventeenth Homily of Clement I and follows on from the quotation given above. It describes the way in which the paradox between the infi-nite and the finite can be resolved by an analogy with cre-ation:

The very subsisting God is therefore One, Who enthroned in more excellent form, is the heart dually controlling both that which is above and that which is below, sending forth from Himself as from a centre, the life-giving and bodiless power, all things with the stars and regions of Heaven, air, water, earth, fire and whatever these be aught else, boundless in height, unlimited in depth, immeasured in breadth, thrice to the boundless stretching forth His life-giving and provident nature. This, therefore, that, starting from God, is boundless in every direction, must needs be the heart holding Him Who is verily above all things in fashion, Who, wheresoever He be, is, as it were, in the middle of a boundless space, being the terminal of the All.[8]

Once again, this is very difficult language yet what he is describing is creation, which is *finite* in so far as it contains finite things, and also *infinite* in terms of the height, depth and breadth of space. In other words, we can know God as within all things and outside all things by seeing his character reflected in his creation. But it is the next paragraph which begins to impinge directly on our quest for Gothic origins:

Taking their origin therefore from Him, the six extensions have the nature of Unlimited things. Of which the one taking its beginning from God is displayed upwards towards the height, another downwards towards the depth, another to the right, another to the left, another in front, another behind. And looking forth on these as on a number equal in every direction, God completes the world in six equal divisions of time, He Himself being the Repose, and having as a likeness, the boundless Aeon that is to be, God being the Beginning and the End. For at Him the six boundless lines do terminate and from Him they take their boundless extension.[9]

What Clement is saying here is that the infinite height, breadth and depth of space and time, may be pictured as six lines which extend for ever and which meet at a point, which both *is* and *is not* because this point represents zero. Today we would call them the *Cartesian co-ordinates*. There is nothing strange or difficult about this picture, which is similar to the description ascribed to Hermes Trismegistus — that God is a circle whose circumference is everywhere and whose centre is nowhere. Yet for our purposes it is truly remarkable because it effectively describes a cube seen as a hexagon and therefore brings us very close to the geometrical figure of the cube-as-hexagon, which was shown to be at the heart of the ground plan of the early Gothic cathedrals and the Cistercian plan of Villard de Honnecourt.

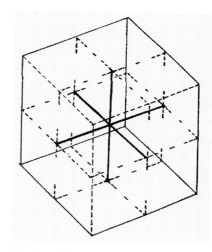

The Cartesian axes meeting at the centre of a cube.

The dark lines at the centre of the cube are the six boundless lines which meet at the centre, the zero point, which *is* and *is not*. These six lines define a cube, which, by its very nature, is made up of eight sub-cubes. It is not hard to recognise that this "zero point" is at the quincunx, or dead centre, of the cube which, as mentioned earlier, was held to be the point of mystical power in the Holy of Holies in Solomon's Temple, from which God spoke to his people. If this cube is slightly adjusted so that the front central point is in line with the quincunx and the rear point, then it turns into the cube-as-hexagon in which the six lines, which divide it into equilateral triangles, become the six boundless lines of the Seventeenth Homily of Clement I of Rome! It seems extraordinary that our apparently unique Gothic ground plan can be derived so easily from this first century text, yet this is indeed the case. For, if we continue to develop this simple geometrical construction, we shall find, via the $1:\sqrt{3}$ rectangle described earlier, that the place-that-is and is-not, the meeting point of the six boundless lines is at the exact centre of the plan, i.e. at the crossing (page 82).

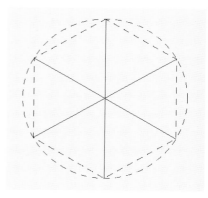

The six boundless lines of Clement I.

Pragnanz — the eye sees a circle that is not there.

If we draw these six lines but stop short of joining them, the eye sees a circle which is not there. The technical, modern name for this is *pragnanz*. It is an optical illusion strangely similar to Abbot Suger's anagogical aesthetic in which the eye sees through the material to the spiritual, from the seen

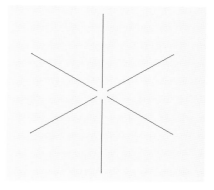

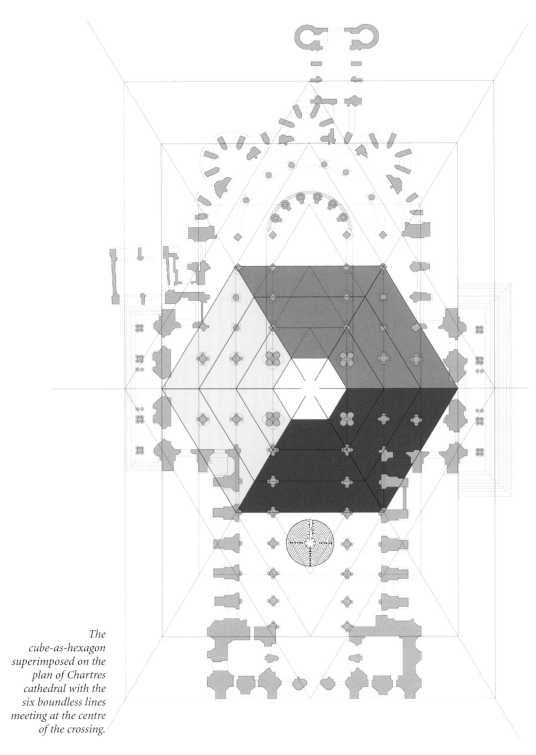

*The
cube-as-hexagon
superimposed on the
plan of Chartres
cathedral with the
six boundless lines
meeting at the centre
of the crossing.*

to the unseen. It is also remarkably similar to the central point of eastern mandalas, or yantras, known as the *Bindu*, through which those who use certain forms of meditation pass into another state of consciousness. At Chartres, consciously or unconsciously, this seems to have been recognised, because the crossing has in recent years, taken the place of the choir and the altar as the main focus and centre of the cathedral. As a result, the choir and altar are relatively dead areas compared with the crossing, which now has a beautiful flood-lit silver altar in the form of the carved base of one of the huge columns, or piers, of the building. Philip Greally, who believes that churches, like people, have chakras and who recently dowsed the whole cathedral for energy points, considered the crossing to correspond to the *heart chakra*. Without being dogmatic about such intuitively perceived energies, it may nevertheless be significant that he felt that the labyrinth was at the sacral centre, the seat of the Life Force, while the choir and altar area contained the *throat, brow* and *crown chakras* (see page 84). To judge by the crowds who continuously wander right round the whole building, the points to which they gravitate seem to be the lower rather than the higher chakras, from the West door to the crossing and particularly the labyrinth. This suggests that they have come more to experience than to understand, for heart rather than head knowledge. This indicates that they have not come there primarily for the mass nor indeed for a detailed explanation of the structure of the architecture or the stories depicted in the stained glass windows, beautiful though they are.

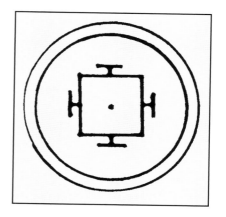

Mandala with Bindu *point in centre.*

The crossing with floodlit silver altar.

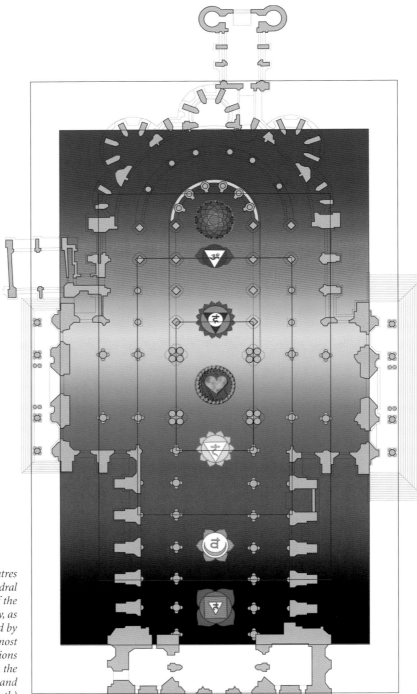

The energy centres of the cathedral match those of the human body, as experienced by dowsers. The most frequented locations coincide with the heart (crossing) and sacral (labyrinth) centres.

CHARTRES: SACRED GEOMETRY, SACRED SPACE

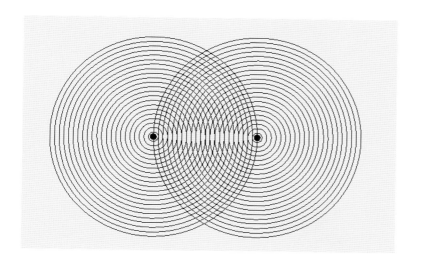

Could the secular modern pilgrims who continue to throng to the cathedral, be drawn to a sacred space laid out and built by skilled sacred geometers and craftsmen, who knew that certain shapes and volumes set up certain vibratory patterns which, while related to music, are more like the silent vibrations of the harmonic overtones, mentioned in Chapter 2? Did they know, or did they subconsciously sense, that the $1:\sqrt{3}$ ratio of the *vesica piscis* sets up a special vibration, related to the subtle body of the human aura and, by extension to the primal tone of creation through the six boundless lines — of the One and of universal Oneness? This could perhaps be inferred from Plato's description of the act of creation, which he says was performed by the Demiurge who, as far as his very cryptic description allows us to interpret, evidently twisted two circles together, one called the Same, and the other called, the Other.[10] This could be taken as a description of the *vesica piscis* and the ripples of energy which come from its two centres.[11] In any case, the *vesica piscis* is known to be the only geometric figure from which all the polygons of creation can be generated.

Did these early masons also realize that the *vesica piscis* was known as the *aureole* and that, as its name indicates, it was symbolic of the light body of Jesus Christ as at his transfiguration and ascension, and also of the human aura — the sheaths of etheric, astral, emotional and mental energy, which surround and protect our physical bodies in the same way as the layers of atmosphere surround and protect our planet?[12]

We must assume that they did, as in the illustration, and that

Concentric Ripples of energy coming from the two centres of the vesica piscis. *Is this the primal tone of creation?*

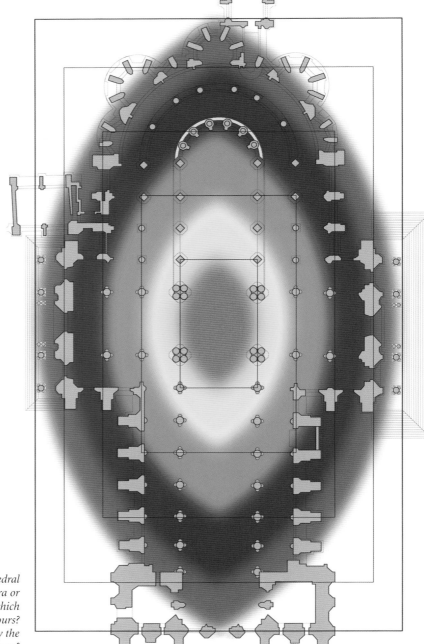

*Does the cathedral
have its own aura or
light body which
resonates with ours?
Is this why the
building affects us?*

just as the Islamic masons knew that the pointed arch helped to harmonize the aura, so they also knew that buildings, if constructed according to the sacred principles of God's creation, had their own auras, which helped to calm, tune and uplift those who came to meditate within them.

Thus, strangely, it would appear that while the Islamic influence was enormous, and the possibility of Gnostic influence cannot be ruled out, the earliest source for the Gothic plan with its symbolism of mystical paradox, may have come from the first Dionysius via Clement I in the first century, despite the confused and legendary nature of the historical evidence.

There was one other theme which came from the very distant past, which was also central to the mystical theology of Dionysius. It was inspirational for Abbot Suger and his stained glass workshops at St Denis and found its perfect expression in Chartres cathedral. This was the theme of the Divine Darkness which, while being closely related to that of the Unknown God, was as distinct from it as the stained glass of St Denis, Chartres and the early Gothic was from all that had preceded it.

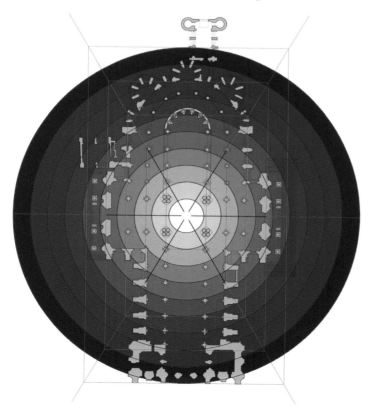

Pragnanz of the six boundless lines can also be extended into the nineness of the celestial hierarchies, discussed in Chapter 7.

Chapter 7

ST DENIS, CHARTRES
AND THE DARKNESS OF GOD

For many people, the idea that there could be a divine darkness, would seem to be a contradiction because in the Judeo-Christian tradition, as in almost every other religion, God is associated with light and darkness with evil. There is scarcely a single hymn, prayer or biblical text which speaks of darkness in a spiritually positive way.[1]

Yet throughout the history of mystical literature, as distinct from doctrinal theology, the concept of the darkness of God has recurred again and again. Why is this?

It would appear to be because, while normal spiritual life is often attended by experiences of the light of God, the higher reaches of the mystic's journey is marked by experiences of the darkness of God. In other words, the concept of the divine darkness comes from the *experience* of the mystical journey, where it is experienced as difficult but not as negative or evil. It is closely linked to the concept of the unknown God (see Chapter 6), and must be understood as another expression of the language of paradox, in which even paradox itself fails adequately to describe what is in essence an indescribable and inexpressible *experience*.

In the mystical theology of Dionysius the Areopagite, these two types of paradox are described one after another in many passages. First let us return to the paradox of knowing and unknowing and in doing so let us note how similar it is to "the-place-that-is" and "is-not" in the Seventeenth Clementine Homily (see Chapter 6):

> Therefore God is known in all things and apart from all things; and God is known by knowledge and by unknowing. Of him there is understanding, reason, knowledge, touch, perception, opinion, imagination,

name and many other things, but he is not understood, nothing can be said of him, he cannot be named. He is not one of the things that are, nor is he known in any of the things that are; he is all things in everything and nothing in anything; he is known to all from all things and to no-one from anything. For we rightly say these things of God, and he is celebrated by all beings according to the analogy that all things bear to him as their Cause.[2]

This language of mystical paradox allows Dionysius to say everything positive *and* negative about our knowledge of God. But of these two ways, the one of affirmation and the other of denial, he says that the way of denial is the more profound. For what God reveals of himself, is not actually himself. We have to go behind the affirmations we make and deny them of God and enter into the mystical experience of the negative, or as it came to be called, *the apophatic way*. Negative, or apophatic, theology is more ultimate. Our denials are truer than our affirmations in relation to God, as he goes on to say:

But the most divine knowledge of God, that in which he is known through unknowing, according to the Union that transcends the mind, happens when the mind, turning away from all things, including itself, is united with the dazzling rays and there and then illuminated in the unsearchable depth of wisdom.[3]

For Dionysius, the archetype and model of this mystical process, was the journey of Moses up Mount Sinai where, after experiencing lights and divine voices, he breaks free of them and plunges into the darkness:

But then Moses breaks free of them, away from what he sees and is seen, and he plunges into the truly mysterious darkness of unknowing. Here, renouncing all that the mind may conceive, wrapped entirely in the intangible and invisible, he belongs completely to him who is beyond everything. Here, being neither oneself nor someone else, one is supremely united to the completely unknown God by an inactivity of all knowledge, and known beyond the mind by knowing nothing.[4]

Dionysius is describing the stages of the mystical journey. He is saying that initially we are led to the experience of God through our mind and through our senses, and that then we are led by the way of unknowing, into sense-deprivation, into a darkness which is mysterious, intangible and invisible, and nearer to the being of God. He goes on to pray that we might all come to experience this darkness, which is superior to light:

> I pray we could come to this darkness so far above light! If only we lacked sight and knowledge so as to see, so as to know, unseeing and unknowing, that which lies beyond all vision and knowledge. For this would be really to see and to know: to praise the Transcendent One in a transcending way, namely through the denial of all beings.[5]

Enough has now been quoted to give the general gist of the central importance of the experience of the divine darkness in the Dionysian mystical theology. However, if we read on to the very next sentence, we encounter a metaphor which takes us suddenly from Moses, in the cloud of darkness atop Mount Sinai, to the craft workshops of Abbot Suger at St Denis. For he likens those who have, as it were, joined Moses in the darkness and are praising "the Transcendent One in a transcending way," to sculptors carving a statue:

Doorway into the darkness.

> We would be like sculptors who set out to carve a statue. They remove every obstacle to the pure view of the hidden image, and simply by this act of clearing aside, they show up the beauty which is hidden.[6]

Is this another way of describing the "anagogical manner," of *seeing through* matter to spirit or pure form which we identified as Abbot Suger's aesthetical principle? I believe it is because there is another passage in which Dionysius speaks about artists and their attitude to pure form, in language which is very reminiscent of that used by Suger:

> It is thus with those artists who love beauty in the mind. They make an image of it within their minds. The concentration and the persistence of their contemplating of this fragrant, secret beauty, enables them to produce

an exact likeness of God. And so these divine artists never cease to shape the power of their minds along the lines of a loveliness which is conceptual, transcendent, and fragrant, and if they practise the virtues called for by imitation of God, it is "not to be seen by men" as scripture puts it.[7]

He goes on to say that if the images, utensils and decorations in the church are contemplated with reverence, then their infinite sacredness will be revealed. This infinitely sacred essence is disguised; it lies within the image as a pure, transcendent form. This is why true artists deliberately "disguise whatever is sacred and virtuously godlike in their mind, imitating and depicting God. They gaze solely on the conceptual originals."[8]

This is so similar to the examples of Abbot Suger's aesthetic given in Chapter 2, that it is hard not to hear his voice speaking through Dionysius. We have moved away from the divine darkness but not from paradox. For by "disguise" he means that which must be removed or "seen through" in order that the hidden sacred and infinite essence may be revealed. This can only be done by what Suger calls "worthy meditation" and by a process of "travelling through" the material to the spiritual. As he said on his new west doors:

Bright is the noble work; but, being nobly bright, the work
Should brighten the minds so that they may travel
through ...[9]

This is so similar to the quotations from Dionysius that it is difficult to doubt the Dionysian inspiration of Suger's aesthetic in the sculptures he commissioned on his new West Porch, and even more in his development and use of stained glass. For in the former he encouraged his great master artist, Godefroid de Claire, to reveal the pure form hidden within the stone, and in the latter he was able to use coloured glass to both reveal and hide the celestial light. In both, he was highly innovative and has been rightly called the foremost creative genius of the New Gothic Style.[10] His position as Abbot of the church, which was believed to have been built on the actual site of the martyrdom of Dionysius himself, and where the martyr's bones were believed to have been interred, gave a huge additional importance to his innovations. To embody the aesthetic of the holy and revered St Denis at the Abbey of St Denis was an honour, a challenge and an inspiration of the highest order. Judging by the reception his renovations received at the dedication in 1144, it seemed that, not for the first time, St Denis himself had answered his prayers and those of most of France.

The extent to which Dionysian thought inspired and permeated all aspects of Suger's epoch-making work can be gauged not only by his Dionysian anagogical aesthetic as described above but also by the actual design of his famous renovated choir. For this and the crypt beneath were divided up into nine semi-circular side chapels in honour of the nine celestial hierarchies described in the Dionysian tract of that name. What is important to note, regarding this particular epistle, is that not only was the number nine of huge cross-cultural significance (see Chapter 1), but that, although they are described as if they were in three groups of three, they were all actually derived from the biblical accounts of mystical experiences. They were not originally meant by Dionysius to be primarily connected to rank, importance, or a *ladder* of mystical ascent to heaven, even if, in the Middle Ages, they were used to justify the earthly feudal hierarchy. They were only originally what he had deduced from mystical experiences described in the Bible. As such they

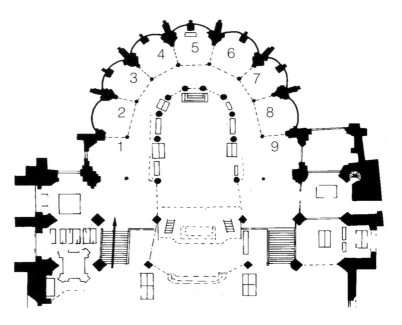

The nine chapels in the Eastern Apse of St Denis, symbolizing the nine celestial hierarchies.

CHARTRES: SACRED GEOMETRY, SACRED SPACE

represented that which every aspiring mystic might expect to experience on his journey as he travelled up Mount Sinai with Moses, to the third heaven with St Paul or to the vision in the Temple of Solomon with Isaiah.[11]

Otto von Simson paints a vivid Dionysian picture at the dedication ceremony of Suger's new choir:

> The two hemicycles of bishops, nine surrounding the Archbishop of Reims in the choir, and nine officiating in the crypt, were undoubtedly meant to represent the nine tiers of angels as described in the Celestial Hierarchy. And the king, as the centre of the procession, represented Christ in the midst of the heavenly hosts. It is likely that the very disposition of the nine chapels around Suger's choir, was inspired by Dionysius.[12]

During the consecration rite, Suger prayed to God, who "invisibly restorest and miraculously transformest the present state into the Heavenly Kingdom ... mayest thou powerfully and mercifully make us and the nature of the angels, heaven and earth, into one republic."[13]

Von Simson goes on to explain the important political link between the heavenly and the earthly hierarchies, which was another powerful reason why the New Style caught on so quickly:

The nine chapels in the crypt of St Denis.

The Dionysian picture of the celestial hierarchy presented not just an idealisation of government, but laid down the design to whose realisation the Christian ruler was committed ... And the astonishing figure of Louis IX, at once king and saint, shows how seriously that demand was taken. Suger's St Denis, the moral values he attributed to its design, attest the public significance of architecture and aesthetic experience generally even more than its artistic achievement.

It is this significance, beyond the purely artistic achievement, that accounts for the extraordinary impression caused by Suger's church. Contemporaries felt immediately that it was designed as an architectural prototype, and seem to have understood likewise that correspondence between the style and decoration of the sanctuary and Dionysian theology which the builder had intended. Precisely because it evoked the mystical archetype of the political order of the French monarchy, the style of St Denis was adopted for all the cathedrals of France and became the monumental expression of the Capetian idea of kingship. It is not surprising, therefore, that in the cathedrals of Paris and Chartres, of Reims and Amiens, the royal theme, evoked not only in the Galleries of Kings but also in the selection of certain Biblical scenes and figures, is completely merged into a Christological one.[14]

I would not wish to detract from or minimize the central importance of von Simson's beautifully expressed political point. However, today, the concept of kingship, let alone divine kingship, has long since fallen into disrepute, and likewise the Catholic Church in France is but a shadow of its former self, the liturgy of the mass no longer expressing the spirituality that many seek. Yet in the Capetian cathedrals such as Paris, Chartres, Reims, Amiens and many others, crowds continue to gather. Why is this? Is it to find out more about their distant past? Do they gather for history lessons? Have these cathedrals become heritage centres? Undoubtedly this is the case to a certain degree. Do the cathedrals also appeal to those interested in cultural and aesthetic matters? I believe that that is also true, up to a point. Yet among those I have met visiting these cathedrals, I have discovered a commitment to a specifically spiritual quest

Alchemical light transforms the darkness.

which, while including the historical and the cultural, also considers a visit to these cathedrals to be more like a pilgrimage.

This has particularly been the case at Chartres where, on a recent visit, I encountered a couple from East Anglia. Since I had been there before and they were there for the first time, I agreed to help show them round. Inside the nave, I began to point out aspects of the architectural design and the stained glass windows, but it soon became apparent that the wife, Lois, was not particularly interested in what I was saying. We fell silent and walked on into the South Transept where she suddenly stopped, put her head in her hands and began to cry. Her husband, Danny, took me aside and explained that she had

The dazzling darkness.

wanted to come to Chartres for years but had been frightened to do so, because she had had an intuition that it might upset her. After a few minutes she composed herself and turned to me and said, "It's about darkness, isn't it? It's about darkness." I said, "Yes, it is." Her husband nodded. After a little while we all walked slowly and silently out of the south door.

It is difficult to assess the effect which Lois' experience had on me, but two things became very clear. Firstly, that Chartres is still a sacred space which, without any religious service taking place, can deeply affect those who visit, so that it is possible to say that the building itself can produce a spiritual experience; and secondly, that the spiritual power of the place is somehow connected to the fact that it is dark. As I reflected on what I had shared with Lois and Danny, all that I remembered having read about the divine darkness in the mystical theology of Dionysius, came flooding back to me. It seemed as though I had only *read* about it, but that Lois had *experienced* it. I began to realize that this might have been the reason why the original builders wanted to build such a huge mysterious building in the first place. Yet I still doubted whether this was the *primary* reason for building, because I thought that if it was, then there would have been some symbolic indication that Dionysius, St Denis and/or his writings had been important to the builders. I did not think there were any such indications because I had not noticed any. However, when I started to look, I found them. I found St Denis himself among the statues of saints and martyrs in the South Porch (page 99). I found numerous types of angels, all nine hierarchies of them, flying around the ceiling of the central arch of the South Porch, above the seated figure of Christ. I discovered that according to the original plan, the cathedral was meant to have had, incredibly, a total of nine

The nine hierarchies in the South Porch above the seated figure of Christ.

The clerestory windows high on the east side of the South Transept showing Dionysius, dressed as Bishop of Paris, giving the Oriflamme to a Templar knight.

spires, only two of which were actually built, but presumably, like the nine doors, it was also in honour of the nine celestial hierarchies.[15]

Most significantly, I discovered one of the huge windows, high up on the east side of the South Transept, devoted to Dionysius, dressed as Bishop of Paris, giving the Oriflamme, the old flag of France, said to have been originally made from the shed blood of the martyr himself, to a Templar knight.[16]

Above and beyond all these confirmations of Dionysian influence, I heard Lois' voice repeating, "It's about darkness." It was this that ultimately convinced me that, even more than in the Abbey of St Denis itself, Chartres embodies the most profound expression of the Dionysian divine darkness that the world has, or probably ever will see. For Chartres, even in summer is always dark, and yet its darkness is by no means ordinary, for it has a *jewelled* darkness. It mediates a dappled, jewelled light which comes through countless windows of the most beautiful and priceless stained glass. Quite apart from the biblical stories depicted in them, or the huge biblical characters who look down as from on high, the colours of the glass itself, the deep reds and blues, create a light which is mystical, which transforms the vast emptiness of the building to a sacred space, as if by some alchemical magic.[17]

It was my experience with Lois and Danny that convinced me that the primary reason why pilgrims still flock to Chartres, consciously or unconsciously, is to experience the beauty of this dark alchemical light. It also convinced me that, quite apart from the historical, political, economic, social and ecclesiastic reasons

The original plan of Chartres with nine spires.

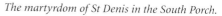

The martyrdom of St Denis in the South Porch.

for its original erection, the primary reason for building it architecturally in the way we see it today, was to express and embody the mystical theology of Dionysius, and to increase the possibility of *experiencing* the darkness of God as on the mystic journey — through the vibrations, the aura, the subtle body of the *building itself*, with or without the liturgy of the mass.

I can no longer doubt that the initial twelfth century impulse to build it the way it is came from a profound knowledge and experience of this mystical spirituality, which remains as hugely effective and affective today as it was for devout Catholic pilgrims seven hundred years ago. Whether you enter as a Catholic, a Protestant, an agnostic, an atheist or a member of another faith, the call of Dionysian mysticism still comes silently to all through the beauty of the stained glass, which bathes the carefully crafted and finely tuned sacred space in mystical light.[18] No one can be entirely free from the possibility that their soul will be touched by this beauty, which speaks of the darkness and of the light of God together; of light in the darkness, of the light behind the darkness. For it intimates and invokes, in an "anagogical manner," the "dazzling rays" which come to us as if from the nine celestial hierarchies, through the darkness of unknowing. The alchemy of the stained glass mediates "the glittering display of the divine glory," and we are encouraged, like Lois, to free ourselves from outer distractions and to enter the depth of our own being.[19] The darkness of the sanctuary still has the power to lead us through the negation of outer, normal, busy-ness and inner confusions to the place-that-is and is-not, at the still point. This is the journey towards the darkness of God in which, paradoxically, we eventually find ourselves nearer to the transfiguring light of his presence:

> I said to my soul, be still, and let the dark come upon you
> Which shall be the darkness of God ...

> ... I said to my soul, be still, and wait without hope
> For hope would be hope for the wrong thing; wait without love
> For love would be love of the wrong thing; there is yet faith
> But the faith and the love and the hope are all in the waiting.
> Wait without thought, for you are not ready for thought;
> So the darkness shall be the light, and the stillness the
> dancing.[20]

The jewelled light creates an alchemy that touches the soul and clarifies the aura. In the darkness we become aware of inner light.

Endnotes

Introduction

1. This is a summary of "Chronology" in Favier p.160.
2. This composite plan is taken from Stegeman 1993. For an alternative, critical assessment of Stegeman see Joly 1999.
3. Sablon, *Histoire de l'auguste et vénérable église de Chartres 1671* in Branner (ed.) p.107–110.
4. Sablon.
5. "When I checked the angle of the sunrise azimuth at Chartres on Midsummer Day, it was 51°58' in 1994 and 51°18' in 1000 BC. At Stonehenge, it was 49°15'." Rigby, p.122.
6. "Having designed the building, Scarlet (the Master Mason) deliberately bent the axes. There was no need to do this, for he had a relatively simple situation to deal with. It could not have been a mistake, for the setting out along the walls of the nave is so accurate there is less than an inch of error in any of the buttresses. Yet at the rondpoint the axis has been moved to the south by a foot, exactly one of Scarlet's Roman feet. There are some twists in the other axes too, forming a coherent and orderly system of sways and bends that belie the possibility of randomness and therefore of error." James, p.103.
7. In ancient and medieval cosmology, the lack of synchronicity between the cycles of the sun and moon was likened to the musical disparity between tuning in octaves and tuning in fifths. It was called the Pythagorean Comma and symbolized the *felix culpa*, the happy fault of the death and resurrection of Jesus Christ. Although it is a very small discrepancy of 1.0136431, at Chartres if we take John James' measurement of 260 Roman Feet for the full width across the transepts, it comes to 3.5 Roman Feet which is very close to the discrepancy between the North and South Porches. For a full explanation of the Pythagorean Comma, see Strachan, 1985, p.50–56.
8. For a detailed examination of the megalithic measurements at Stonehenge, see Strachan, 1998, p.206–209.

9. By a strange coincidence, Professor Thom's Megalithic Rod of 6.8 feet, is the same as the Greek Fathom, i.e. 2.0726 metres. There are seven Roman Feet in a Greek Fathom. Dividing John James' 260 Roman Feet gives us thirty-seven Greek Fathoms plus one Roman Foot. Since the Megalithic Rod (MR) is the same as the Greek Fathom, this is also thirty-seven MR plus one Roman Foot. This extra foot is well within the difference between the two axes which create the Pythagorean Comma. For this unpublished metrological insight, I am grateful to my late colleague, Anne Macaulay.

Chapter 1

1. The Gothic style evolved through an "immanent or an internal" process which had "nothing to do with the Crusades," Frankl, p.220. *See also* Wilson.
2. Islamic influences form "part of the prehistory of Gothic architecture" Conant, p.106. Also: "it is only from Eastern sources that the Western architects can have acquired the pointed arch which was to become the symbol and chief mark of the Gothic style." Harvey, p.88.
3. "Most architects gained their knowledge from Arab science." Gimpel, p.98–101.
4. "...what the pointed arch called for ... was a more sophisticated use of geometry, and this could only have come from the East, for knowledge of Euclid was preserved in the Moslem East and lost in the Dark Ages of the Christian West." Atroshenko and Collins, p.35.
5. Bowie, p.125.
6. Warren, p.59f.
7. Harvey, John, "The Origins of Gothic Architecture: Some Further Thoughts," *The Antiquaries Journal,* No. 48, 1968, p.97.
8. Pennick, 1994, p,97. See also *The Archaeological Journal* 3, 1846, p.277.
9. Pennick, p.85. See also *The Archaeological Journal* 3, 1846, p.277.
   Other early examples include: Cluny III 1088–1121 (Bannister Fletcher); St Etienne

Caen 1100 (Paul Frankl); Gloucester Cathedral wall arch 1100 (Paul Frankl); Moissac "the front vault" 1120–25 (Paul Frankl 1962 and Conant 1959); Moissac cloister, but may have been changed; Monrienval ambulatory 1122; Church of Holy Sepulchre 1149.

10. Crosby, p.19.
11. St Bernard, Letter 80, p. 110–18.
12. Shah p.166–93.
13. Armstrong, p.76.
14. "There was no doubt a certain interchange of ideas between Sufism and Christianity. The Knights Templar, for example, almost certainly made intellectual contacts with the Sufis." Encyclopaedia Britannica Vol 21, p.374. Also "many Templars were soaked in the culture of the East and some may well have come into contact with the Sufi schools." *See* William Anderson in Picknett and Prince, p.163.
15. Hancock, p.96. For example, if "modern archaeologists have never been permitted to work there" [on the Temple Mount], how can Hancock be entirely certain that the Templars "used their occupancy of the Temple Mount to conduct quite extensive excavations"?
16. Wasserman, p.273–76.
17. Southern, p.172–73.
18. *See* Read 2001; Barber 1994; Riley-Smith 1990.
19. "Chartres remained a centre for the diffusion of Arabic science in the West until well into the twelfth century — and not for diffusion only, but for the most successful absorption of this science into the body of Christian learning which was achieved at any time before the thirteenth century." Southern, p.193.
20. Rosenthal, 1992.
21. Malouf, p. 104–33.
22. For most scholars this argument from silence would be considered weak. Nevertheless there have been well known influential secret traditions in history, notably the Pythagoreans and the Freemasons. As far as the Templars are concerned it is the contention of this book that the evidence lies ultimately in the architectural not literary sources. For a sympathetic assessment of the secrecy of medieval masons see Hiscock, p.97–100.
23. Richmond, p.44.
24. "Mameluke Sultans restored both sides of the mosque and added two bays on either side of the Crusader porch (1345–50)." Murphy-O'Connor, p.67.
25. Otto von Simson is correct when he claims "The Cathedral of Sens is the first Gothic cathedral." But he, I believe, is wrong in his belief that it is built according to ad quadratum design and according to simple musical ratios. Von Simson, p.142f.
26. But not Graham Hancock. Among illustrations on p.120.
27. I am grateful to architect and colleague Robert Chalmers for pointing this out to me.
28. Sablon; Branner, p.107–110.
29. Ean Begg, *The Cult of the Black Virgin,* Penguin, 1996, p.5.

Chapter 2

1. Southern, p.164f.
2. Ruskin, p.165f.
3. Pothorn, p.64, 68.
4. Briggs, p.7.
5. Viollet-le-Duc, p.392.
6. Lethaby, 1994.
7. Lethaby, 1904, p. 169.
8. Morgan, p.16.
9. Morgan, p.18.
10. Abbot Suger, p.63.
11. Abbot Suger, p.47.
12. For a sceptical interpretation of Suger's use of the writings of Dionysius the Areopagite, *see* Grant, p.24.
13. Plato, 9f.
14. Bakhtiar, p.104. *See also* Critchlow.

Chapter 3

1. Dunlop, p.13f.
2. Von Simson, p.101.
3. Villard de Honnecourt, Plate 41, p.92.
4. Robinson (ed.) p.6 and p.68f; Ferguson, p.35f.
5. Swaan, p.51.
6. Swaan, p.51.
7. Hufgard, p.9–40.
8. Cantor, p.409.

Chapter 4

1. Fernie and Crossley, p.229.
2. "The Ka'ba ... contains in embryo , everything expressed in the sacred art of Islam," Burchkardt, p.3.
3. Critchlow
4. Burckhardt, p.9–14.
5. Pennick, p.104–13.

Chapter 5

1. Bligh Bond and Lea, 1981, p.99.
2. James, p.96.
3. James, p.97.
4. Fideler, 1993, p.284f.
5. Fideler 1987, p.20–24.
6. "The fish is also the symbolic designation of the Piscean Age, and consequently the Vesica is the dominant geometric figure for this period of cosmic and human evolution, and is the major thematic source for the cosmic temples of this age in the west, the Gothic cathedrals." Lawlor, p.33.

Chapter 6

1. Brankovic.
2. Pelikan, "The Odyssey of Dionysian Spirituality." See Luibheid, p.21f.
3. Pseudo-Dionysius, p.141.
4. Brankovic, p.6.
5. Clement I of Rome, Homily 17. See Bligh Bond and Lea Part II, 1985, p.107–8.
6. Quite suddenly the influence of Dionysian concepts began to emerge in the twelfth century. "Abbot Suger of Saint-Denis borrowed some ideas from Dionysius to explain the symbolism of light in the basilica he had built." Also there were other monks influenced by Dionysius, "the most important of whom belonged to the monastery of Saint-Denis." Leclercq, "Influence and non-influence of Dionysius in the Western Middle Ages." See Luibheid, p.27.
7. The scholarly consensus claims that Bernard's mysticism was of light not darkness, that it followed Augustine and was "innocent of any Dionysian taint." Yet Bernard made a distinction between what was appropriate for his monasteries and the new secular cathedrals. It is significant that the windows of Sens were enlarged after Bernard's death, that Suger at St Denis was always an exception and that at Chartres, the close friendship which Bishop Geoffrey de Levès had with Bernard *and* Suger is expressed by the combination of the Bernardine Plan with the Dionysian jewelled darkness of the stained glass. *See* Louth, 1976, p.2; von Simson, p.145–56.
8. Bligh Bond and Lea, 1985, p.109.
9. Bligh Bond and Lea, 1985, p.109.
10. Plato, *Timaeus*, 35. *See* Michell, p.86.
11. "Is this merely a pattern of pebbles, of vibration, or is it also a metaphor for love, for the power of shared limits, and for the creative act itself?" Doczi, p.139.
12. Aureole: "Latin aura, 'gold,' connected with aurora, 'dawn.' Thus, through the image of the radiating light of the sun at dawn, the aureole is the radiating mantle enveloping specifically the body as opposed to the head of a divine being." Whone, p.17.

Chapter 7

1. The one biblical exception to this is, most significantly, at the dedication of Solomon's temple, when Solomon prays to God who "dwells in thick darkness" (1Kings 8:12; 2Chr. 6:1). This is probably an example of the same tradition as the ascent of Moses up Mount Sinai into the darkness of God. Was it for this reason that the Holy of Holies was always in darkness?
2. Dionysius the Areopagite, *The Divine Names VII:872 A-B. See* Louth 1989, p.88.
3. Dionysius the Areopagite, *The Divine Names. See* Louth 1989, p.88.
4. Dionysius the Areopagite, *The Mystical Theology 1:3. See* Luibheid, p.137.
5. Dionysius the Areopagite, *The Mystical Theology. See* Luibheid, p.138.
6. Dionysius the Areopagite, *The Mystical Theology. See* Luibheid, p.138.
7. Dionysius the Areopagite, *The Ecclesiastical Hierarchy. See* Lubheid p.226.
8. Dionysius the Areopagite, *The Ecclesiastical Hierarchy. See* Lubheid p.226.
9. Abbot Suger, *See* Panofsky, p.47.
10. Mâle, p.155–86.
11. Dionysius gives the first triad of angelic beings as the seraphim, cherubim and thrones; the second as dominions, powers and authorities, and the third as principalities, archangels and angels. Louth 1989, p.47–50.
12. Von Simson, p.139.
13. Von Simson, p.140.
14. Von Simson, p.141.
15. James, p.75.
16. The identity of this knight is uncertain. He is "traditionally regarded as the marshal of Philip Augustus who died in the crusades." Favier, p.154.
17. Simon Trethewey, the stained glass craftsman writes: "The science of alchemy as evolved

under Islamic influence, incorporated a system of seven colours." He concludes his unpublished essay *The Alchemy of Light:* "The production of glass and its colouration has had a direct and practical link to the science of alchemy in its aspect of craft experience. The ancient recipies for glass that have survived verify this by virtue of the fact that they are sometimes heavily couched in alchemical terms and by the fact that these same recipes rely upon metals as their primary agents for bringing about the manifestation of colour. The production of glass can also be associated with alchemy in its deeper spiritual aspect. The symbolic qualities of its production and the material itself being significant and parallel to the alchemical process. The extraction of the noble metals from the impure ores in the furnace is paralleled by the transformation of glass by fire and the incorruptible light of gold is paralleled by the quality of glass, to become light without itself changing."

18. John James believes the "fine tuning" was very fine indeed, to the extent that the masons deliberately bent the axes slightly. He has discovered that the rondpoint at the altar has been moved to the South by one Roman foot. This tilt can be observed looking east from the west door. He believed it was designed to avoid exact, dead symmetry, to let the building breathe and to "open a window into the Infinite." This agrees exactly with the theology of the immeasurable, mystical God put forward throughout this book. In musical terms, perhaps this would be equivalent to vibrato and to the Pythagorean Comma; the slight alternation of tone formed by the discrepancy between tuning in octaves and tuning in fifths. It may also be equivalent to the difference between the South Porch which sits on the platform and the North Porch which extends to two steps down, for John James has found this discrepancy runs throughout the building. James, p.103f. *(See also* Introduction).

19. Louth, 1989, p.106.

20. Eliot, "East Coker," p.28.

Bibliography

Abbot Suger, *Abbot Suger on the Abbey Church of St Denis and its Art Treasures,* (Trans. E. Panofsky) Princeton 1979.

Archaeological Journal 3, 1846.

Armstrong, Karen, *Islam,* Phoenix, 2001.

Atroshenko, V.I., and Collins, Judith, *The Origins of the Romanesque,* Lund Humphries, 1985.

Bakhtiar, Laleh, *Sufi: Expressons of the Mystic Quest,* Thames and Hudson, 1976.

Barber, Malcolm, *The New Knighthood,* Cambridge UP, 1994.

Begg, Ean, *The Cult of the Black Virgin,* Penguin, 1996.

Bligh Bond, F., and Lea, T.S., *Gematria,* RILKO–Thorsons, 1981.

—, *The Apostolic Gnosis, Part II,* RILKO–Thorsons, 1985.

Bowie, Theodore (ed.), *The Sketchbook of Villard de Honnecourt,* Indiana University Press, 1959.

Brankovic, Branislav, *Saint Denis, un saint, une legend,* Castelet, Paris, ISBN 2-908555-60-3.

Branner, Robert (ed.), *Chartres Cathedral,* Norton, New York 1969.

Briggs, Martin, *Cathedral Architecture,* Pitkin, 1990.

Burchkardt, Titus, *Art of Islam,* World of Islam Festival Publishing Company, 1976.

Cantor, Norman, *Medieval History: The Life and Death of a Civilization,* Macmillan, 1963.

Clement I of Rome, Homily 17. *See* Bligh Bond, F, and Lea, T.S, *Part II,* 1985.

Conant, K.J., *Carolingian and Romanesque Architecture,* Penguin, 1959.

Critchlow, Keith, *Islamic Patterns,* Thames and Hudson, 1976.

Crosby, S.McK., *The Royal Abbey of Saint Denis,* MMOA, New York, 1981.

Dionysius the Areopagite, *The Divine Names VII:872 A-B. See* Louth 1989.

—, *The Ecclesiastical Hierarchy. See* Luibheid.

—, *The Mystical Theology 1:3. See* Luibheid

Doczi, Gyorgy, *The Power of Limits,* Shambala, 1981.

Dunlop, Ian, *The Cathedrals' Crusade,* Hamish Hamilton, 1982.

Eliot, T.S. *Four Quartets,* Faber and Faber, 1976.

Encyclopaedia Britannica, Vol 21, 1969.

Favier, Jean, *The World of Chartres,* Thames and Hudson, London 1990.

Ferguson, Peter, *The Architecture of Solitude,* Princeton UP, 1984.

Fernie E. and Crossley P. (eds.), "A Beginners' Guide to the Study of Architectural Proportions and Systems of Length," *Medieval Architecture and its Intellectual Context,* Hambledon, 1990.

Fideler, David, *Jesus Christ, Sun of God,* Quest Books, 1993.

—, (ed.) *The Pythagorean Sourcebook and Library,* (Trans. by K.S. Guthrie), Phanes Press, 1987.

Frankl, Paul, *Gothic Architecture,* Penguin, 1962.

Gimpel, Jean, *The Cathedral Builders,* Pimlico, 1993.

Grant, Lindy, *Abbot Suger of St Denis,* Longman, 1998.

Guthrie, K.S., *The Pythagorean Sourcebook and Library. See* Fideler.

Hancock, Graham, *The Sign and the Seal,* Heinemann, 1992.

Harvey, John, "The Origins of Gothic Architecture: Some Further Thoughts," in *The Antiquaries Journal,* No. 48, 1968.

Harvey, John, and (ed.) Joan Evans, *The Flowering of the Middle Ages,* Thames and Hudson, 1998.

Hiscock, Nigel, *The Wise Master Builder,* Ashgate, 2000.

Hufgard, M. Kilian, *Saint Bernard of Clairvaux, A Theory of Art Formulated from his Writings,* Edwin Mallen, Lampeter 1990.

James, John, *The Master Masons of Chartres,* West Grinstead, Australia 1990.

Joly, Roger, *La Cathédrale de Chartres avant Fulbert,* Editions Houvet, 1999.

Lawlor, Robert, *Sacred Geometry,* Thames and Hudson, 1982.

Lethaby, W.R., *Architecture, Mysticism and Myth,* Solos, 1994.

—, *Mediaeval Architecture,* London 1904.

Louth, Andrew, *Denys the Areopagite,* Morehouse-Barlow, 1989

—, *The Influence of Saint Bernard,* SLG Press, Oxford 1976.

Luibheid, Colm (trans.), *Pseudo-Dionysius. The Complete Works,* SPCK, 1987.

Mâle, Emile, *Religious Art in France, The Twelfth Century,* Bollington Series, Princeton UP, 1992.

Malouf, Amin, *The Crusades through Arab Eyes,* Al Saqi Books, London 1984.

Michell, John, *City of Revelation,* Garnstone, 1972.

Morgan, B.J., *Canonic Design in English Mediaeval Architecture,* Liverpool UP, 1961.

Murphy-O'Connor, Jerome, *The Holy Land, An Archaeological Guide,* Steimatzky and OUP, 1985.

Panofsky, E. *Abbot Suger on the Abbey Church of St Denis and its Art Treasures,* Princeton, 1979.

Pennick, Nigel, *Sacred Geometry,* Capal Bann, 1994

Picknett, Lynn and Prince, Clive, *The Templar Revelation,* Corgi, 1998.

Pothorn, Herbert, *A Guide to Architectural Styles,* Phaidon, 1982.

Pseudo-Dionysius. *See* Luibheid.

Read, Piers Paul, *The Templars,* Phoenix, 2001,

Richmond, R.W., *The Structural History of the Aksa Mosque,* OUP, 1949.

Rigby, Greg, *On Earth as it is in Heaven,* Rhaedus, Guernsey, 1996.

Riley-Smith, Jonathan, *The Crusades,* Athlone, 1990.

Robinson, David (ed.), *The Cistercian Abbeys of Britain,* Batsford 1998.

Rosenthal, Franz, *The Classical Heritage in Islam,* Routledge, 1992.

Ruskin, John, *The Seven Lamps of Architecture,* 1880, Dover, 1989.

St Bernard, *The Letters of St Bernard of Clairvaux* (trans. Bruno Scott James) Sutton Publishing, 1998.

Shah, Idries, *The Sufis,* Anchor-Doubleday, 1971.

Southern, R.W., *The Making of the Middle Ages,* Hutchinson, 1967.

Stegeman, Charles, *Les Cryptes de la Cathédrale de Chartres et les cathédrales depuis l'epoque gallo-romaine,* Société archéologique d'Eure et Loire, Chartres 1993.

Strachan, Gordon, *Christ and the Cosmos,* Labarum, Dunbar 1985.

—, *Jesus the Master Builder,* Floris Books, Edinburgh, 1998.

Swaan, Wim, *The Gothic Cathedral,* Omega, 1988.

Trethewey, Simon, *The Alchemy of Light.* Unpublished essay.

Viollet-le-Duc, *Lecture on Architecture,* (tr. B. Bucknall), London 1881, Vol I.

Von Simson, Otto, *The Gothic Cathedral,* Princeton UP, 1974.

Warren, John, "Cresswell's use of the theory of dating by the acuteness of the pointed arches in early Muslim architecture," *Muquarnas Vol VIII,* Leiden 1991.

Wasserman, James, *The Templars and the Assassins,* Inner Traditions, 2001.

Whone, Herbert, *Church, Monastery, Cathedral,* Compton Russell Element, 1977.

Wilson, Christopher, *The Gothic Cathedral,* Thames and Hudson, 1994.

Index

akbar jahd 28
Aksa Mosque, El 23f, 29–31
Amiens Cathedral 94
André de Gundomare 26
André de Montbard 26
Archambaud de Saint-Aignan 26
Aristotle's *Categories* 27
Augustine, St 46

Bakhtiar, Laleh 38, 40
Bernard, St (Abbot of Clairvaux) 20,
    26, 31, 39, 43, 48, 52, 79
Bernardine Plan 45
Bindu point 83
Black Virgin 33
Bligh Bond, Frederuck 61
Briggs, Martin 36

Capetian cathedrals 94
Carnutes Druid Grotto 10
Cartesian co-ordinates 80f
chemise (of the Virgin Mary) 34
Cistercian church/plan 43–46,
    48–50, 59, 63f, 67
Clement I, Pope 74, 78
—, Seventeenth Homily of 78–81, 88
Cloud of Unknowing 78
Constantine, Emperor 21
Constantinople 21
Creswell, K.A.C. 18
Crusades, Crusaders 14, 17f, 21f, 25f,
    28, 60, 67, 72

Denis Abbey, St 20, 27, 38, 43, 87, 92–94
Denis, St, Bishop of Paris 30, 67, 74,
    79, 92, 97, 99 *(see also* Dionysius
    the Areopagite)
Dionysius the Areopagite *(see also* St
    Denis) 27, 30, 32f, 40, 74, 76–79,
    87–92, 97, 99
Dionysius, Pseudo- 74f, 77f
Dome of the Rock, the 22f, 58f
Durham Cathedral 19
Dyad 68

Edessa, fall of 30
Enneagram 27
Ezekiel's Temples 57

Fernie, Eric 53, 65
Fulbert, Bishop 9

Geoffroy Bisol 26
Ghazali, al- 22
gnosis 27
Godefrey Bisol 26
Godefrey de Saint-Omer 26

Hermes Trismegistus 81
Holy Sepulchre, Church of the 9, 21, 23
Honnecourt, Villard de 17, 18, 43,
    45f, 48, 81
—, Cistercian plan of 48–50, 59, 63f,
    67
Honorius II, Pope 26
Hugues de Payens 25f

Ieou, Book of 61, 74
Ismailis 27

James, John 61–63, 65, 70
John of Salisbury 9

Kaaba 57f
Knox, Ronald 53

Lalys (mason) 19
Laon Cathedral 28, 58, 67
Lethaby, William 37, 45, 65
Levès, Geoffrey de, Bishop of
    Chartres 20, 31

Mandala 83
Mary as Ever Virgin 69
Mary as *Sedes Sapientiae* 32f
Mecca 57
Megalithic Rods (MR) 13
Megalithic Yards (MY) 13
Morgan, B.G. 37, 65
Morris, William 36
Moses 89f, 93
Muhammad 23
mukkahmmas arch 23f, 32, 43

Neath Abbey 19

Our Lady Under the Earth 32f

Paris Cathedral 45, 59, 94
Paul, St 76, 93
Payen de Montdidier 26
Payens, Hugues de 25f
Pistis Sophia 61, 74
Plato 37f, 46
—, Academy of 38
Platonism 37
Pothorn, Herbert 36
Pseudo-Dionysius 74f, 77f

quadratum, ad 59f
Quadrivium 35

Reims Cathedral 94
Richard de Granville 19
Roman arch 24
Roman Foot (RF) 62
Roral 26
Ruskin, John 36

Saladin 30
Seljuks 21
Senlis Cathedral 44f, 59, 67
Sens Cathedral 31, 43–45, 59, 67
Seven Liberal Arts 35
Simson, Otto von 93
solar-lunar double axis 12

Solomon, Temple of 35, 46f, 54, 56f, 60, 81, 92
Stonehenge 11f
Sufi(s) 22, 25, 27f, 32f, 40, 42, 50, 60, 67, 72
Suger, Abbot 20, 31, 37–39, 43, 45, 48, 52, 74, 79, 81, 87, 90–94
Swaan, Wim 45f

Templars 25f, 28, 30–33, 40, 42, 58, 60, 67, 72, 74, 99
Templar Cross 31
Temple Mount 23, 26, 58
Temple of Solomon 35, 46f, 54, 56f, 60, 81, 92
Thierry of Chartres 9
Thom, Alexander 13
Triad 68
triangulum, ad 59–61, 64, 67f, 72
Triple Goddess 32

vesica piscis 68, 70–72
Viollet-le-Duc 36
von Simson, Otto 93

William of Calais 19
William of Conches 9

Photographic Acknowledgments

With thanks to the following for the photographs and diagrams on the pages indicated:

Agence Photographique de la Réunion des Musées Nationaux 75
Bridgeman Art Library 32, 41, 71 (photograph), 76, 97
G. Lewes 37, 54, 90, 95
C. Maclean 23, 24 (top)
Oliver Perceval 8, 11, 18, 24 (bottom), 25, 51, 52, 59, 61, 62, 64, 65, 66, 73, 84, 85, 86, 87, 101
Gordon Strachan 3, 12, 13, 20, 21, 29, 31, 33 (left), 34, 69, 83, 96

Floris Books

For news on all our **latest books,**
and to receive **exclusive discounts,**
join our mailing list at:

florisbooks.co.uk

Plus subscribers get a FREE book
with every online order!